P9-CRE-285

Contents

RYAN'S DOG
Ringo

Written by Marie Gibson • Illustrated by Richard Hoit

Written by Marie Gibson
Illustrated by Richard Hoit

© 1995 Shortland Publications Inc.

04 03 02 01 00 99
11 10 9 8 7 6 5 4

Published by Shortland Publications Inc.

Distributed in the United States of America by

a division of Reed Elsevier Inc.
500 Coventry Lane
Crystal Lake, IL 60014
800-822-8661

Distributed in Canada by

PRENTICE HALL GINN
1870 Birchmount Road
Scarborough
Ontario M1P 2J7

Printed through Bookbuilders Limited, Hong Kong.

ISBN: 0-7901-1001-6

Chapter 1

Ryan Lambert heard the van pull up. That's Aunt Beth, he thought, back from the city with Greg. It was two weeks since he'd seen them. Two weeks since Greg had gone into the hospital for the operation that was supposed to get him walking again. Had it worked? Or was it going to be a failure, like the other one? He wouldn't ask just yet.

Ryan ran to the front of the house to meet them. Aunt Beth was already wheeling Greg down the ramp to the sidewalk. Why wouldn't she wait for him to help?

"Ryan!" called Greg. "We're home!" Greg's smile spread across his face, but he was pale, with dark smudges under his eyes. His thatch of straw-colored hair hung over his forehead. He needed a haircut, and he looked even thinner than when he went away.

No one had ever believed the twelve-year-old boys were twins. They looked so different. Ryan had dark gray eyes and brown hair, like their dad. He was solid and strong.

People who had known their mother said Greg took after her. He was tall and thin, with blond hair and pale blue eyes. Before his accident, he'd been the fastest runner in the school.

"Great to have you home, Greg," Ryan said. He hugged his brother.

"Don't be rough, Ryan," Aunt Beth snapped. She used her tight grip on the wheelchair to turn Greg away from him. Ryan pulled back guiltily. Nothing he did was right.

Aunt Beth was Dad's older sister. She used to be fun when she first came to live with them. That was five years ago – after their mother died. But when Greg had his accident, things changed. She insisted on doing everything for him and she had no time for anyone else.

Just then, Rachel Stein from the boarding kennels strolled past on the opposite side of the road. She was walking her black Labrador, Paddy. Her faded shorts and T-shirt contrasted with her tanned arms and legs. Her dark ponytail flipped across her freckled cheeks as she bent to restrain the dog.

"Want to come for a walk, Ryan?" she called. She didn't cross over. No one brought a dog near Greg. Everyone knew that he'd been attacked on his bike by a dog, and how he'd hit his head and injured his spine. That was last year and he hadn't walked since. Now he panicked if a dog came anywhere near. So did Aunt Beth! But then, she'd never liked dogs anyway.

Ryan crossed the street to pat the big, friendly Labrador. Paddy wagged his tail and licked Ryan's hand.

"I'd better not come," said Ryan. "Greg just got home from the hospital. Anyway, there's a party at gymnastics tonight." He looked over his shoulder and saw his aunt struggling up the gravel path with Greg's wheelchair. She'd almost reached the steps. "I have to go."

Ryan wished they had a ramp. Dad suggested it, but Aunt Beth refused. She said Greg wouldn't need a wheelchair for long. He'd be walking again in no time. Everyone hoped she was right.

Ryan got there just in time to help her up the steps.

"It's the final gymnastics night tonight, Aunt Beth," Ryan said when everything was unloaded and they had Greg settled in front of the TV. "Can you come?"

"Oh, Ryan! Really!" she said, nodding toward Greg. "How can I? Your father will have to go with you."

"But I've cooked dinner, and the table's set. They're presenting the awards tonight. And I've won the trampoline cup."

"What about Gregory?"

"He can come, too. His friends ask about him all the time. They'd like to see him."

"Sometimes you're very thoughtless, Ryan. How do you think Gregory feels seeing all his friends doing gymnastics when he can't even walk? He won that cup last year, and now he's stuck in a wheelchair!"

"But..."

"Now, Ryan." Dad came in and closed the door. "Not arguing with your aunt already, are you?" He hugged Greg and kissed Aunt Beth's cheek. "Great to have you both home. Ryan's a pretty good cook," he joked, "but I'd like a change from hamburgers and hot dogs."

Ryan frowned at the floor. Things aren't going to get any better. Aunt Beth still does things only for Greg. She doesn't care about anyone else. Dad doesn't appreciate anything I do, either, he thought.

When it came right down to it, Ryan was sick of everything revolving around Greg.

They'd cancelled their last trip because Aunt Beth thought Greg would feel self-conscious if strangers stared at him in his wheelchair. She didn't ask Ryan what he wanted to do.

Dad had bought a computer. He said it was for both

boys, but it was kept in Greg's room. Ryan used it whenever he wanted to, but he always felt he had to ask first.

Worst of all, just before the accident, Ryan had been promised he could have a dog. He'd saved up two years' birthday money, and most of his allowance. They'd all gone to see the litter of German shepherd pups, and he'd chosen the one he wanted. He was going to call him Ringo.

But it was a German shepherd that crashed into Greg, so that was the end of that. Even before the accident, Ryan knew Aunt Beth didn't like dogs much. Afterward, she wouldn't discuss them at all. Ryan asked Dad about it.

"Leave it a while," Dad said. "Beth has so much extra work looking after Greg; it's not fair to make any more problems for her."

Ryan should have known it was a waste of time expecting her to go with him to gymnastics that night. It would have meant getting a sitter for Greg. But Greg didn't like anyone except Aunt Beth taking him to the bathroom and getting him into bed.

As it turned out, Dad had to go back to work, so Ryan went to the gymnastics award presentation alone. That's nothing unusual, he thought. But it felt wrong sitting by himself with the cup he'd won and no family to say, "Congratulations!" No one to give him a hug or shake his hand.

Ryan didn't even stay for the food. He went home early.

Greg was still up. His eyes looked red, as though he'd been crying, but he smiled when Ryan came in.

"Let's see your cup," he said, holding out his hands. He rubbed it with his fingers and inspected the engraving. "Look, there's my name from last year." He smiled up at Ryan.

It would be Greg's name there again this year if it weren't for that dog, thought Ryan. I can't believe how he's handling this. If it was me, I wouldn't want to see the stupid cup, much less touch it!

Ryan's lips tightened as he tried to smile back. He took the cup and put it on the shelf.

"How about a game of cards?" suggested Greg.

Ryan shook his head. "Nah, I'm off to bed," he said. He felt guilty. Playing cards was one of the few things they could do together now.

But he'd had to go to the awards banquet on his own. It was only fair that Greg should put up with some disappointment, too.

The boys used to share a room. They talked for hours at night after the light was out. Now there wasn't enough

space in the one room for two boys, a wheelchair, and all the gear Greg needed. Aunt Beth made Ryan move out into the sunroom.

Ryan felt a kind of loneliness. He missed the brother he used to have. The one he raced and wrestled with. The one he beat at swimming. The one who beat him in gymnastics.

He missed having turns being first with Aunt Beth and Dad, too. Now it was always Greg who had first choice with everything. I suppose he should, thought Ryan, because he's lost almost everything else. But it still hurt.

There was something that hurt even more, and that was not being able to have Ringo. It was all very well for Greg. He'd never been that crazy about dogs, but Ryan loved them. He could have put up with everything else if he had a dog to look after.

Chapter 2

The next afternoon, Ryan walked home from school with Rachel. They stopped and talked outside the kennels.

"Come in and see Sylvester," said Rachel.

"Who's Sylvester?"

"Mr. Harley's Dalmatian. He came in yesterday and he's a beauty."

Ryan didn't need any persuading. He went in and put the back of his hand up to the mesh for the dog to sniff. It wagged its tail. Ryan reached in and patted its spotted coat. Sylvester *was* a beauty.

"He likes you." Mr. Stein had walked up behind Ryan. "He's nervous with everyone else. Would you like to exercise him out in the yard?"

"Would I!" shouted Ryan. He dumped his bag and slipped through the gate. He snapped Sylvester's leash onto his collar and took him out to the yard. The dog pranced beside him. He moved so fast, Ryan could hardly keep up. Mr. Stein watched through the fence.

Ryan was flushed and panting by the time he put Sylvester back in the kennel. Mr. Stein waited for him. "You like dogs, don't you?" he said.

Ryan nodded.

"Do you want an after-school job – helping out at the kennels?"

Ryan nodded again.

"What about your dad? Maybe you should ask him first."

"He won't mind," he said. "Neither will Aunt Beth." And I don't care if they do, he told himself.

"What will they pay you?" Dad asked that night. Ryan hadn't thought to ask. The money wasn't important – not just then.

For the first night in ages, he didn't miss having Greg to talk to. He didn't even think about him. He remembered only the excitement of working with the big, spotted dog.

Every afternoon from three-thirty until five o'clock, Ryan scrubbed kennels, exercised dogs, and fed them. He groomed cats and washed food bowls.

Cats had never interested him before, but now he

liked their welcoming meows, and their warm purring when he patted them. One half-grown, striped cat was especially friendly. She rubbed around his legs and leaped onto his lap whenever he sat down. She bumped her head under his chin and wrapped her tail around his neck. He missed her when he went home.

Ryan thought he'd like to have a cat. Maybe if they wouldn't let him have a dog...

He sat at the table in silence that night.

"What are you thinking about, Ryan?" Dad asked. "You haven't been this quiet since before you started at the kennels."

"A cat. Could we have a cat or a kitten?" There was no way to approach the subject delicately, so he blurted it out. They'd probably say "No" anyway. "Mr. Stein said you can get kittens free from the animal shelter," he went on. "It would still need shots. But I've got the money I was keeping for Ringo..." He stopped. He shouldn't have said anything about the puppy. It always caused trouble. But this time no one took any notice.

"Don't see why not," Aunt Beth said, and went on calmly eating her dinner. "A kitten would be best. It's hard to get an older cat to settle into new surroundings."

Something went thump inside Ryan's stomach. His soup wobbled in his spoon and spilled back into his bowl.

Aunt Beth had said "Yes" to something he wanted!

The next night after dinner, Rachel went with Ryan to the animal shelter. They peered into the rows of cat cages. On the opposite side of the enclosure were the cages for the dogs. Poor things, he thought. No one wanted them.

"Look," said Rachel. "There's a dog like Paddy. Why is he here? He must belong to someone."

Ryan wished he'd come to get one of the dogs, but he didn't dare look at them. He knew what happened to dogs at the animal shelter when no one gave them a home. He didn't want to think about it. Anyway, he'd come for a kitten.

It was hard to choose. Rachel liked the fluffy, gray one, but Ryan pointed to a striped, orange kitten spinning in circles after its tail.

"I'll take that one," he said.

"What are you going to call her?" asked Rachel, as the woman in charge lifted the kitten out of the cage. Ryan thought of Ringo, but that reminded him of the German shepherd pup he couldn't have, and anyway, the name wouldn't fit a girl kitten very well.

"Zip," he said. "She moves so fast, I'll call her Zip."

As Ryan reached home with the kitten cuddled in his arms, he saw Greg watching out the window.

"Let's see," called Greg when they got inside. Ryan unhooked the kitten's needle claws from his sweater and lowered her onto Greg's lap.

"You hold her while I pour her some milk and organize her bed," Ryan said. He put Zip's bed beside his own and set up a box of cat litter nearby. He brought the kitten into the bedroom and showed her the litter box.

"That's so we don't have any puddles on the carpet," he said.

Ryan fed Zip night and morning, and spent most of his spare time playing with her.

"A waste of time," Aunt Beth said, as Ryan dragged along a scrap of crumpled paper tied to a piece of string. Zip crouched behind the table leg and pounced as it fluttered past.

"I'm teaching her to hunt," he said.

Every time Ryan came in the door and called, "Kitty, kitty!" Zip came running. She rubbed around Ryan's legs and purred. While they watched TV after dinner she curled up on Ryan's lap and slept.

Now it didn't matter that Greg came first with Aunt Beth, because Ryan came first with Zip. He hardly noticed that Aunt Beth spent all her time with Greg. When he thought about it, he supposed she must be helping him with his exercises. No one else was allowed to.

If Greg was using the computer when Ryan wanted it, he just shrugged his shoulders and went off to his bedroom with a book – and Zip.

He stopped wondering if they were going away on vacation, or if they'd stay home again because of Greg. Ryan wanted to stay home now that he had a kitten.

Ryan knew that even if he wasn't important to anyone else, he was important to Zip. Zip was his kitten.

At least she was his for a week, until a spell of warm weather came.

Chapter 3

"Would you like a few extra hours work on the weekend?" Mr. Stein asked on Friday. "Everyone's going away now that the weather's improving. We have so many bookings, I'm putting in new dog runs."

Ryan not only worked all weekend, but did an extra half hour each weekday.

"I've fed Zip for you," said Greg, when Ryan got home late on Wednesday evening. "She was starving!"

"Thanks," said Ryan, as Zip leapt into his arms and purred around his face. "I'll probably be late tomorrow, too. Can you feed her for me again?"

"You were the one who wanted this cat, Ryan," Aunt Beth said from the kitchen, where she was spooning up the casserole for dinner. "Don't think you can push the responsibility of feeding her onto Gregory."

Ryan made a face behind her back.

"It's no trouble," Greg said, glancing sideways at her.

Ryan saw the deep lines down beside Aunt Beth's mouth. Her eyebrows were drawn together. She looked worried. Maybe Greg hadn't made much progress with his walking. At times like this no one dared argue with her. All the same, Greg went on, "I like looking after Zip. It gives me something to do."

So from then on, Ryan gave Zip her breakfast, and Greg gave Zip her dinner. It suited everyone – especially Zip.

On Saturday afternoon Ryan came home late again.

"Zip!" he called. "Kitty, kitty, kitty. Here, kitty!"

Zip didn't come. Ryan called again. Still no cat.

The steady beeping of a computer game came from Greg's bedroom.

"Greg," said Ryan, looking around the door, "have you seen the cat?"

"What?" Greg looked up from his game. "Are you looking for Zip? She's here." Greg leaned back, and Ryan saw the kitten curled up on his brother's knee.

"Here, Zip," said Ryan.

The kitten half-opened her eyes and looked at Ryan.

"Meow," she said. Then she shut her eyes and curled up sleepily on Greg's knee. She purred while Greg scratched behind her ear.

That night Zip slept on Greg's bed. Ryan missed her.

He'd gotten used to the warm, furry body curled up near his pillow, and the friendly rumble when the little cat purred.

The next morning he heard Aunt Beth talking to Dad.

"It's really good for Gregory to have a pet," she said. "I thought a cat would be a nuisance, but Zip gives him something to think about."

It seemed that Greg had taken over Zip now, as well as everything else.

"You can feed the cat this morning, Greg," Ryan snapped as he marched out the door. "I'm late."

With the upset over the kitten, Sunday had gotten off to a bad start, and it didn't get any better.

Ryan was late for work. He arrived at the kennels to hear ferocious barking in the exercise yard.

A dogfight! Paddy and Sylvester! Ryan raced around to the yard. Paddy was chained to the fence, but he'd gotten in at least one good bite. Sylvester had blood dripping from his ear. Both dogs snarled from between curled lips and gleaming fangs. Sylvester lunged at Paddy from every angle. He was determined to get his own back.

Ryan helped Rachel drag the hose across the yard. They turned the jet onto both dogs.

"Heel, Sylvester!" shouted Ryan. The Dalmatian was startled by the cold water. He forgot about his enemy long enough to obey the command.

"What happened?" Ryan asked, as he returned Sylvester to his cage and examined the damaged ear.

"Just as I got Paddy chained up, Sylvester started barking. I would've left him until you got here, but you were late, and I couldn't stand the noise. So I brought him out to the yard myself." The fuss was over, but Rachel still trembled. "When he saw Paddy, he pulled away from me. I couldn't hold him!"

Sylvester had always behaved badly with Rachel. Ryan wasn't surprised there'd been trouble.

"Sylvester's going home today," Rachel went on. "Mr. Harley won't be pleased to see that ear when he comes to get him."

Rachel's dad wasn't pleased, either. He gave them a good telling-off for having two dogs in the enclosure at once.

"I'll have to take him to the vet," said Mr. Stein. "See if you two can carry on here sensibly while I'm gone." He glared at them as he piled Sylvester into the van.

"Sorry you got the blame, too, Ryan," said Rachel, shivering in the cold wind. She'd gotten a good drenching from the hose. Her long, straight hair clung in dark strings to her neck, and her goose-pimpled arms stuck out from the sleeves of her wet shirt.

"Doesn't matter," he said. "It was going to be a bad day, anyway." He looked at her. "You're cold. You'd better go in and get changed."

Ryan was coiling up the hose when a car stopped outside. A woman came in with a small dog on a leash. It yapped and leaped up at her. In seconds it had all the other dogs barking as well.

"Sorry." The woman looked embarrassed. "Dad never did get around to teaching Trixie any manners." At the sound of her name, the little dog sat still with her head on one side, listening. What a mischievous little face, thought Ryan. He'd never seen anything like her before.

"What breed is she?" he asked.

The woman looked even more embarrassed. "I have no idea – a bit of everything, I think. Dad got her from the animal shelter."

"Like my cat," said Ryan. Then he remembered. Like Greg's cat. "Come to the office," he said. "I'll check on your reservation." Ryan looked at the chart. There was no entry for Trixie. "Haven't you got a reservation?" he inquired.

"No. It's an emergency. My father went into the hospital, suddenly, this morning."

"I'm afraid we don't have any vacancies," said Ryan. "Can't you keep her until your father gets home again?"

"I live in an apartment, and we can't have animals." The woman's eyes became watery. Don't tell me she's going to cry, thought Ryan. "My father's not expected to live very long. I suppose we'll have to find a permanent home for her."

Ryan looked down at Trixie. Poor little thing. Just as well she didn't understand.

"Mr. Stein has looked after her before," the woman said. "I'm sure he'll agree to have her. Just for a couple of days – until we decide what to do." She pushed the leash into Ryan's hand, plonked fifty dollars on the desk, and disappeared out the door.

Ryan didn't like little dogs. They were scatterbrained, silly things. German shepherds had been his favorite ever since he'd watched them loping along like wolves at a police dog demonstration. They were magnificent.

Since he'd known Sylvester, Ryan liked Dalmations, too. In fact, he just plain liked all big dogs! He looked down at Trixie. She wagged her tail, just the tip, and whined hopefully.

"What are we going to do with you?" said Ryan, trying to speak kindly. Trixie's floppy brown ears stood up. She listened. "We don't have an empty kennel. Even when Sylvester goes home, that run is reserved for another dog." Trixie jumped up on Ryan and scraped her front paws down his bare legs.

"Ow! Good dogs don't do that!" Ryan lifted one hand to push her away. Before he even touched her, she yelped and cowered away from him.

"Poor Trixie. I know you didn't mean to scratch," he said. "Did you think I was going to hit you?" He held out his hand and waited. After a minute she crept forward and sniffed his fingers. He stroked her head and patted her dusty coat. She needed grooming. When he rubbed around her ears, he felt tufts of matted hair.

"We'll have to fix that," he said.

He'd clipped off the worst bits and was combing out the rest when Mr. Stein came back with Sylvester.

"Not as bad as we thought. Just a scratch, really," said Mr. Stein. Then he stopped. "What's she doing here?"

Ryan started to explain.

"But we don't have anywhere to put her, Ryan," Mr. Stein interrupted. "You know that." He stood there, staring at her. "The last time we had her, she yapped so much, she started all the other dogs barking. I had to take her into the house. Then she stole things off the table and shed hair all over the furniture.

"She gave me that cute look one day, so I took her down to the beach for a run. What did she do? She dashed out onto the road and chased cars."

He frowned and continued. "You can't do anything with a dog like that! I said I'd never have her back!"

"But there's nowhere for her to go!" Ryan objected.

"There's always the animal shelter."

"Dad! You can't do that!" Rachel appeared in the doorway in dry clothing. "You know what'll happen to her if we send her there!"

"Yes. Well – that has nothing to do with us, does it?" Mr. Stein said.

Ryan looked down at her. She wasn't much of a dog, but she didn't deserve that. It wasn't her fault she had nowhere to go.

Mr. Stein tried to stand firm, but with both Rachel and Ryan against him, he didn't have much of a chance. By the time he led Sylvester back to his cage, he agreed to give Trixie five days – until her fifty dollars ran out.

Chapter 4

"Let's take her to obedience school," said Rachel. "If you're under sixteen, you can take your dog for nothing." She looked at the calendar. "It's on tonight. Seven o'clock at the park." Ryan wasn't too enthusiastic, but he didn't have anything else to do.

There were over thirty dogs at the park by the time Ryan and Rachel got there with Trixie. They were all sizes and breeds, but there was nothing that looked like her.

A boy about Ryan's age had a German shepherd – a real beauty. Its thick coat was dark gray, and it had a pale throat and chest. It turned its head and flicked its pointed ears to pick up every sound. Ryan's breath caught in his throat. He couldn't breathe for wanting that dog.

"Come on." Rachel tugged his arm. "We've got to line up over there."

"You take her," he said. It wouldn't have been so bad if she'd been a poodle or a terrier or a breed with a name.

He wasn't going to be seen with a mutt.

Rachel and Trixie lined up with the others, and the instructor arrived. She was a tall lady named Mrs. Mansfield. She moved with a fast, gliding walk, just like the golden Afghan hound at her side. They were alike in other ways, too. The hound's long, flowing coat floated out behind him like Mrs. Mansfield's long, flowing skirt. His silky ears fluttered at either side of his nose, like Mrs. Mansfield's wavy, auburn hair.

"Let me introduce all of you to Julius," she said in a commanding voice.

"Sit, Julius." Julius sat.

"Stay, Julius." Julius stayed while his mistress inspected the lineup of dogs. She spoke to each dog, but ignored the owners.

Mrs. Mansfield returned to the obedient Julius, who demonstrated how a dog should walk at heel behind its trainer. The two of them, hair and clothes streaming behind, did a graceful circle and stopped. Everyone tried to copy.

A few dogs completed their circle fairly well, but the rest were disasters. Some pulled on their leashes, dragging their owners this way and that. One snarled and lunged at any dog that came near. Two grabbed their leashes between their teeth and took their owners for the walk.

Ryan looked for the handsome German shepherd. Where was he? Over there. Sitting down. Refusing to move. All the other dogs had to detour around him. His owner jerked his leash and gave him a shove with his foot, but the dog still wouldn't move.

Everyone glared at the boy because shoving dogs is not allowed. How embarrassing! Just as well Mrs. Mansfield wasn't watching! Trixie is probably doing something stupid, too, Ryan thought. He looked around for her. Rachel had her out in front of everyone. Mrs. Mansfield bent down and patted the little dog.

"Good dog, Trixie," Mrs. Mansfield said. "You did well."

What a surprise! Ryan felt almost proud of the little dog. She wasn't such a mutt, after all. He wished he'd been the one to take her out into the park. One other dog got a pat and a "Good dog" from Mrs. Mansfield. It was a collie belonging to a man in a wheelchair.

Dog school was full of surprises!

The dogs did some more walking in circles, then Mrs. Mansfield showed everyone how to make their dogs sit. After that, it was time to go home.

"Practice everything we've done tonight, and I'll see you all Wednesday," Mrs. Mansfield said, as they left the park.

"Wasn't Trixie great!" said Rachel.

Ryan nodded. "Yes, but wasn't that German shepherd a beauty!"

"He looked good, but he was stupid," snapped Rachel. "I couldn't be bothered with a dog like that." She marched ahead of Ryan. He hurried to catch up. Trixie trotted obediently at Rachel's side until a big, noisy car roared past. She yanked her leash out of Rachel's hand and raced after it.

"Trixie! Heel!" Rachel shouted. But Trixie didn't come back until the car had escaped around the corner. When she finally returned, she slunk in behind Rachel, crawling the last yard on her belly. She knew she'd done wrong.

"Bad dog!" scolded Rachel, shaking her finger. Trixie tucked her tail between her legs and whimpered.

"I think she's sorry," said Ryan.

"I should hope so," said Rachel angrily. Then her face crumpled with worry. "She could have been run over. How can we stop her?"

———

Obedience school again tonight, Ryan thought, as he hurried up the sidewalk after work on Wednesday.

Before he reached the front door, he heard sobbing. It came from Greg's bedroom window. He wasn't surprised. Greg often had red eyes when Ryan came home.

"Put that stupid cat down and try again, Gregory!" Aunt Beth's exasperated voice interrupted the crying. "You know what the doctor said. You have to do your exercises – but if you won't even try..." Then Greg's door slammed, and Aunt Beth's footsteps marched down the hall to the kitchen.

When Ryan got inside, he peeped in at her. She was peeling potatoes at the sink. Her mouth made a straight line, and a frown ridged her forehead. She looked angry. Ryan watched her more closely. She looked tired and worried, too. He tiptoed away to Greg's room.

Greg sat on his bed. He cuddled Zip and buried his face in the orange fur.

"What's wrong, Greg?"

Greg looked up suddenly. His pale face was streaked with tears. "I'll never walk," he whispered. "They say I will, but they're only trying to make me feel better." He sniffed. Ryan passed him a tissue and sat beside him.

"How d'you know?"

The sniffing went on. Zip's purring joined in. Ryan reached over and stroked the kitten's ears.

"Zip's your kitten," Greg changed the subject. "I shouldn't have taken her."

Any other time, Ryan would have agreed with him. Not now. Greg's miserable face made Ryan feel he'd been selfish about the kitten.

"I don't mind if you have her," he lied. He put an arm around his brother's shoulders. How thin he was. No wonder – he ate hardly anything. Ryan felt him shaking as the sobs tried to escape again.

"I do try, Ryan," Greg insisted. "I concentrate on all the things the doctor said, but Aunt Beth knows it's impossible. I can tell. She's so tense and nervous when she tries to help me stand, I seize up. I can't do anything! Then she gets upset and that makes it worse. Today she got really angry."

Greg's anxious fingers shredded the tissue into confetti. "She knows I won't ever walk," he whispered.

"Why don't you forget about it for today," suggested Ryan. Then without thinking, he added, "How about coming to obedience school with Rachel and me tonight?"

What a stupid thing to say to a boy who couldn't walk anymore because of a dog! Of course he wouldn't want to go.

Greg sat very still. He didn't speak for awhile.

At last he said, "You'd have to push me, and I'd feel stupid sitting there in a wheelchair."

"No stupider than the man with the collie that did so well on Sunday," said Ryan.

Greg looked up. The misery had gone out of his eyes.

It was replaced by surprise. "Is there someone in a wheelchair with a dog?" he asked.

Ryan nodded. He didn't want to say any more in case he put Greg off.

"But Aunt Beth might not let me go. You'll have to ask her."

"We won't ask. We'll just tell her we're going. Like we used to before..."

Ryan sounded a lot braver than he felt. He'd have sneaked Greg out the door without saying anything if it wasn't for those dumb steps. They were so steep. He'd need help to get the wheelchair safely down to the sidewalk.

For the hundredth time, he wished for a ramp.

Chapter 5

Before Ryan gathered up enough courage to tell Aunt Beth he was taking Greg to obedience school, she made an announcement of her own.

"I've got to go out tonight and your dad's working late," she told Ryan. "You'll have to stay with Gregory." The boys glanced at each other across the table. Ryan wondered where she was going. She never went anywhere these days.

Greg opened his mouth to speak. Ryan frowned and shook his head. "OK," he said.

"I thought you were going to the dog school." Aunt Beth eyed him suspiciously.

"Yes, I was, but I won't leave Greg on his own."

Greg hid a smile behind a forkful of potato. Ryan noticed he'd eaten almost everything on his plate. Maybe that's because we're going out, he thought. Sitting around at home all the time must be really boring.

As soon as their aunt went out, Ryan hurried to the phone. "Rachel?"

"Yes. Is that you, Ryan?"

"Yes. Listen, I can't meet you at your place. Could you come here? I need a hand with something."

"What is it?"

"You'll find out when you get here. G'bye."

He put the phone down and grinned. "That's one problem out of the way." He rubbed his hands.

"Why does *she* have to come here?" Greg frowned. "Why does she have to come at all? We don't need her."

"Because it was her idea, that's why. Anyway I do need her – to help get you down the steps. I'll be in enough trouble if we're caught going to the park. Imagine what would happen if I tipped your wheelchair over! I'm not ready to risk it. Are you?"

Greg's mouth turned down stubbornly at the corners.

"Now what's wrong?" asked Ryan.

"I don't want a girl helping me. I'll feel stupid."

"It's that or stay home."

"But you want to go, though," argued Greg.

"Yes, of course I do. But I'm not going to risk you getting hurt!"

A knock at the door interrupted the argument. It was Rachel.

"Tie Trixie to the fence, please," Ryan told her. "I need your help to get Greg down the steps."

Rachel's eyes popped. "Are you going, too, Greg?" she said. "Are you allowed?"

"Of course I am. I'm not a baby. I can decide where I go! It's only my legs that don't work," he answered angrily. "Not my brain!"

Before Greg changed his mind, Ryan wheeled him to the top of the steps. He shut Zip inside the house and took the wheelchair handles. Rachel took the front.

They bumped down the first step. Ryan's arm muscles bulged as he pulled back to keep the wheelchair from getting away.

Rachel looked up at Greg. "It's all right," she said. "We won't drop you." A smile split her freckled face. Greg tried to smile back at her, but without much success.

On the way to the park, Greg wouldn't look at Trixie bounding along beside him. Ryan knew how nervous he felt, though.

He watched his brother's shoulders hunch and his hands make sudden grabs at the armrests when the dog got too close. Rachel didn't seem to notice.

"I can't believe you're coming with us, Greg," she said. "I thought you didn't like dogs." Thank goodness she didn't say anything about being *frightened* of them.

"You can't really call Trixie a dog, can you?" Greg answered back, and he made himself grin.

He knows he's silly to be frightened of a little thing like Trixie, thought Ryan.

"Watch it, or I'll tell her to lick you!" teased Rachel.

When they got to the park, Rachel handed Trixie's leash to Ryan.

"Your turn tonight."

"I'd better look after Greg," he said.

"I can look after Greg," she insisted. She gave Ryan a push. Greg didn't object, so Ryan tugged on the leash and lined up with the others. When Mrs. Mansfield inspected the dogs, he was sure she had an extra smile and a pat for Trixie.

At the end of the lesson, Mrs. Mansfield stopped to talk to Ryan. "That's a clever little dog you have there," she said. "There are beginners' obedience trials next month. You should enter her. I'm sure she'll be ready."

Ryan was about to tell her that Trixie wasn't his dog and that he might not have her next month, when she said. "But it will depend on when she's due to have her pups."

"Pups?"

"Yes," laughed Mrs. Mansfield. "You know – little dogs!" Then she stopped laughing. "You didn't know, did you!" She rolled Trixie onto her back and ran her hand over the dog's stomach. "She's due to deliver in about two weeks, I should think."

———

Ryan was last to leave the park. He'd been standing there, staring at Trixie. He didn't even see the boy with the German shepherd as he raced across the grass. Not until the big, gray dog lunged at them. Trixie stood her ground and yapped fiercely. Ryan swept her up out of the way. That gave the other boy just enough time to regain control of his dog and drag him out through the park gate.

Ryan put Trixie down. "That was close," he said, "but you saved us, didn't you?" He knelt down and patted her. "We thought *you* had no manners. What about him!

"And what about these puppies, Trix?" he went on. "They're the real problem. What are we going to do about them? It'll be hard enough to find a home for you, without worrying about puppies. And tomorrow's your last day."

He walked slowly across the park to where Rachel and Greg waited.

"You'd better ride home with Greg, Trixie," Rachel

said, when she heard about the puppies. Greg hesitated for a minute, then he patted his lap, and she jumped up.

Ryan and Rachel took turns pushing the wheelchair.

"How many d'you think she'll have?" asked Greg.

"It doesn't matter how many," answered Ryan. "Rachel's dad doesn't even want her. He certainly won't have her *and* her puppies."

Rachel and Ryan dragged and heaved Greg up the steps and inside. Trixie followed them. Zip leaped onto the bed. It was safer there. She glared down at Trixie and hissed. Trixie backed off.

"You're a sensible little cat," Ryan said, patting her. "You know all about dogs – even little ones."

Greg got out the cards. "What should we play?"

Aunt Beth got back early. She heard the three of them in Greg's bedroom, laughing and shouting about who'd won the last game. They knew she was home when the front door banged shut.

Ryan grabbed Trixie and pushed her under the bed. "Stay!" he whispered. She'd only just learned "Stay." He wasn't sure she'd remember.

"Don't say where we've been," Greg quickly whispered to Rachel.

Aunt Beth came into the room.

"Hello, Aunt Beth," chorused the boys.

"Hello, Miss Lambert," said Rachel.

Aunt Beth looked around. This was the first time there'd been laughter in this room for ages. There hadn't been any visitors for awhile, either. She'd kept them away, in case they stared at Greg or said something to upset him.

"What's all the noise?" she asked suspiciously.

"Just cards, Aunt Beth," said Greg. Ryan looked at his brother's lively smile. He's having fun, he thought. He still can't walk, but he's having fun.

Rachel left a few minutes later. After saying good-bye in a loud voice, she crept around the house to Greg's window. Greg wheeled himself out to the kitchen and kept Aunt Beth busy, while Ryan passed Trixie out to Rachel.

"Good dog, Trixie," he whispered. She squirmed with pleasure. She knew all about "good dog."

Rachel waved as she jogged off down the road, with Trixie prancing at her side.

They'd all decided not to tell Mr. Stein about the pups just yet.

"We'll deal with *that* problem when we have to," said Rachel.

Chapter 6

The next day was the first day of summer vacation. Ryan would be working full time.

That morning, another fifty dollars arrived in the mail. There was a note with it saying "For Trixie" on one side, and a short message on the other. "My father died this morning. I'll contact you soon."

Ryan looked across at Rachel. That gives us another five days. Five days before we have to decide what to do.

"If I knew where that woman lived, I'd send the money back and tell her to come and take her dog away!" said Mr. Stein as he crumpled up the envelope and threw it in the wastepaper basket. "I don't even know her name!" He glared at Trixie and stomped off to feed the other dogs. Ryan went with him to help.

"But, Dad," Rachel raced after them. "Trixie doesn't bark anymore at night. She doesn't cause any trouble. And Mrs. Mansfield says she's the smartest dog at the school."

Her father stopped and turned around. "I know why she doesn't bark anymore," he said. "It's because you sneak her into your bedroom every night! I know what's going on! But one thing I *would* like to know is, where's the next fifty dollars coming from?"

"I'll pay." Ryan was surprised to hear himself say it. Trixie wasn't his dog. And he had to remind himself how he felt about "little dogs." He'd almost forgotten.

"You don't *earn* much more than that," said Mr. Stein.

"I know," agreed Ryan. He dropped some dog food into each dish in the row of cages.

"Oh well..." Mr. Stein shrugged his shoulders. "It's up to you how you spend your money. I'm not worried." He picked up the hose to begin cleaning out the cages.

He won't be worried until he finds out about the pups, thought Ryan.

That was sooner than anyone expected – even Mrs. Mansfield.

———————

When Ryan got back from the kennels, Zip was waiting for him on the doorstep. Aunt Beth was out back, weeding the garden. The house was quiet. Where was Greg? Ryan headed for his brother's room. An odd sound came from the other side of the door. Ryan listened. It was a mixture of a grunt and some loud breathing.

"Greg?" he said softly. "You all right?"

The noise stopped. "Is that you, Ryan?" Greg panted.

"Yes. What's wrong?"

"I need a hand. Come in."

Ryan opened the door and found Greg slumped on the floor beside his bed. The wheelchair stood in the middle of the room.

"What happened? Did you fall?" Ryan put his hands under Greg's arms and lifted. How light he was!

"Sort of," said Greg. "I tried to get out of bed and into the chair by myself. The brake wasn't set. It shot away over there."

"Let me help you," said Ryan, when he'd gotten his brother safely back on the bed.

"No – that's the whole point. I've got to start doing things by myself. Aunt Beth won't even let me try. She always does everything for me." He stared down at his skinny ankles where they poked out from his sweat pants. His fingers wound themselves into the sheet crumpled up behind him.

"D'you think you're ready to try by yourself?" Ryan asked quietly.

"It's no good with Aunt Beth helping me!" Greg blurted out. "She wants me to do things her way, and when I can't, she gets mad and says I'm not trying! She says I'm being difficult! Does she think I want to stay in this wheelchair the rest of my life?" Greg's voice quivered and his shoulders started to shake.

"Well," said Ryan, trying to be reasonable, "what do you want to do?"

"The first thing I want is to get from my bed to the wheelchair and back again – on my own."

"Why don't you try it again? I won't try to help unless you ask me to."

"All right." Greg sounded more confident already. "Push the chair over here where I can get at it. That's right, but don't put the brake on! I'll do that."

Greg leaned over, dragged the chair around, and pulled the brake lever. Then he turned sideways to the chair and grasped the nearest armrest with one hand. He reached behind him for the other armrest and swung himself backward into the chair. Ryan folded his arms to stop himself from reaching out to help.

"There! I knew I could do it! Aunt Beth always parked the chair out of reach because she thought I'd fall. I'll show her!"

"Listen," said Ryan, "the phone."

"Let me," insisted Greg. He pushed the wheels of his chair and sent it through the doorway into the hall.

"Hello. Greg Lambert speaking." He listened for a moment. A smile spread across his face. "I'll tell Ryan! We'll be right over!" He put the phone down and turned to his brother. "Rachel's taking Trixie to the beach for half an hour before dinner. I said we'd go, too."

"What do we say to Aunt Beth?" Ryan looked doubtful.

"We say we're going to the beach. That's what we used to say." Greg spun his chair toward the back door. "Aunt Beth!" he called. "Can you come here and give us a hand, please?"

Aunt Beth appeared in the doorway. "What is it?"

"We need you to help us down the steps," he said.

"What are you going to do?" She looked puzzled.

"We're going to the beach with Rachel. We won't be long. Half an hour, maybe. It's just these stupid steps." Greg spoke casually. Ryan waited for Aunt Beth to hit the roof.

"You don't need to go to the beach now," Aunt Beth said. Her lips tightened, and her fingernails dug into the palms of her hands.

"No, but we want to."

"If you wait a while, I'll take you in the van," she said.

Ryan wondered how Greg would get around that.

"We don't want to go later on. We want to go now, and Ryan will push me."

Ryan was astounded at the way Greg kept his cool.

He didn't nag. He didn't complain. He just insisted on doing what he wanted to do.

"What if something goes wrong?" Aunt Beth demanded.

"Like what?" Greg smiled. Nothing was going to ruffle him, and he was going to the beach.

Aunt Beth had no answer. Reluctantly she helped them down the steps. The last thing she did was tuck a blanket over Greg's knees.

"It could be cold down there," she said. Greg started to push the blanket away, but Ryan frowned at him so he left it there. There was no point in upsetting Aunt Beth when they'd gotten their own way.

As Ryan wheeled Greg down the road, he looked back at the house. Someone peered out from behind the curtain.

"Aunt Beth's watching," Ryan said. They both waved, but no one waved back.

Chapter 7

At one end of the beach was a place for people to exercise their dogs. When they got there, the sand was dry and soft. Too soft for Greg's wheelchair.

"This won't work," said Rachel, when they had gotten stuck for the third time.

"I shouldn't have come." Greg sounded disappointed. "If you pull me back onto the sidewalk, I'll wait there for you."

"We'll pull you back onto the sidewalk, all right," said Ryan. "Then we'll go down by the water. It's low tide. The sand's packed there."

"Dogs aren't allowed there." Greg looked up at Ryan. "What about the dogcatcher?"

"He won't be here at this time of day," Rachel said confidently. Ryan and Rachel pulled together to drag the wheelchair out of the soft sand.

At the other end of the beach, they ran along the hard

sand. They took turns pushing Greg. Trixie bounced alongside. Sometimes she raced off on her own to clear away the sea gulls. When they got to the far end, they turned and looked back. They grinned at the great swooping tracks made by the wheelchair.

"I'm glad Aunt Beth can't see those!" said Ryan. He looked at his watch. "Hey, we'd better get back. You said something about half an hour, Greg. It's almost that now." He turned the wheelchair and began pushing it toward home.

A piece of driftwood floated toward them on the

incoming tide. Trixie grabbed it before a wave washed it back out to sea. She dropped it at Rachel's feet. Rachel picked it up and threw it along the beach. After retrieving it, Trixie dropped it in front of Ryan again and again. Soon, he got tired of it, too. "You'll be next, Greg," he said.

They laughed when Trixie dropped it in front of the wheelchair. "It's no good putting it there," said Greg. "I can't reach it." He patted his knee. "You'll have to put it up here."

Trixie picked up the stick, hopped up onto Greg's footrest, and dumped the stick in his lap.

"Good dog," he said and patted her head. "Mrs. Mansfield said you were." He threw the stick. Trixie raced after it, barking a high, shrill bark. She came back and repeated her trick.

"Listen! What's that?" said Rachel.

A motorcycle zoomed down from among the dunes at the far end of the beach.

"It's the dogcatcher," said Ryan. "He'll get us for having Trixie here. It's a thirty-dollar fine!"

"No he won't," muttered Greg. "Here, Trixie," he called. She leapt up onto his footrest again and put her stick on his lap. He dragged the blanket from the back of his chair and draped it over Trixie and himself. She was completely hidden. "Stay, Trixie," he whispered.

The dogcatcher skidded around in front of them and covered them with a spray of damp sand.

"Where's the dog?" he demanded.

"Dog?" said Rachel innocently.

"Yes! I heard a dog barking and there's no one else here, is there?"

"No, there isn't." Rachel looked around, searching for whoever had a dog on the people's end of the beach.

"I can't see a dog, either," said Greg.

"Sorry we can't stay and help you look," Ryan apologized. "We're late getting home already."

Ryan knew the dogcatcher was watching them suspiciously as they pushed the wheelchair up onto the sidewalk. Before they got out of sight, he saw the man staring at their tracks in the sand. Ryan began to laugh.

"It's not funny," grumbled Rachel. "We nearly got caught!"

"The dogcatcher is looking at our tracks," he said. "He'll see one set of wheelchair tracks, two pairs of footprints, and some dog tracks that stop suddenly and go nowhere. I bet he's puzzled."

They were all laughing when the dogcatcher's bike whizzed past on the road. Trixie struggled to get free and chase it.

"Stay!" commanded Greg, as he held her still. "Give me her leash," he said. Ryan untied it from the back of the wheelchair. "We'd look silly if she got caught chasing the dogcatcher!" Greg said. He snapped the leash onto her collar, and tied the other end to his armrest.

They left Rachel and Trixie at the kennels. Greg was still grinning about the disappearing dog tracks when they got home – late.

———

Aunt Beth rushed out to meet them. "Where've you been?" she demanded. "I was worried sick!"

"Sorry, Aunt Beth," said Ryan. "We went farther than we meant to."

"You're so irresponsible, Ryan," she panted, as she helped him heave Greg's chair up the steps. "That's the last time you take Gregory with you! Anything could have happened!" She wheeled him down the hall to the kitchen.

"Like what?" said Greg.

"Just... anything!"

Dad appeared at the door. No one heard him come in.

"Greg? Did I hear you arguing with your aunt?"

"It's not Gregory's fault," said Aunt Beth. "It was Ryan. He took Gregory away and didn't bring him back. I bet he didn't even think about all the dogs they have racing around the beach."

"That's not fair!" Greg's voice got louder. "I'm as much to blame as Ryan for being late!"

Ryan watched an angry frown cloud Dad's face.

"I think you boys should go to your rooms now, while I discuss this with your aunt." He spoke slowly and deliberately.

Greg swung his chair around and rolled through the door. Ryan followed him. When he turned to close the door, he looked back into the kitchen. Dad glared at him. Aunt Beth's lips trembled. She looked like she might cry.

As Ryan passed his brother's door, Greg called softly. "Ryan. Come in here."

Ryan glanced behind. The kitchen door was still shut. "What d'you want?"

"Why is Aunt Beth so crabby lately? She's mad about everything. Before this happened," he slapped the side of his wheelchair, "we used to spend the whole afternoon at the beach and she didn't worry. Now she won't let me out of her sight. And why was she picking on you tonight?"

Ryan shrugged his shoulders. "She's been like that for ages. I wanted her to come to the gymnastics club the other night and bring you, too. She got angry about that. She said..." he hesitated. He didn't want to upset Greg, but this seemed to be the time for honesty. "She said I wasn't being fair, expecting you to watch everyone doing gymnastics when you were stuck in a wheelchair. She thought you'd be embarrassed if other kids stared."

"She was probably right – then. I felt rotten the other night when Rachel had to help get me down the steps. I nearly said I wouldn't go. But I don't care now – not much anyway. It was fun down at the beach this afternoon."

The kitchen door opened and Dad strode into Greg's room. "I think we'd better have a talk." He didn't sound so angry, but he still looked serious. "There are a few things you seem to have forgotten. Six years ago, Aunt

Beth was a well-paid nurse at a city hospital. She enjoyed her job and was very good at it. Then, of course, everything went wrong for all of us. First, your mother..." Dad's voice came out husky – the way it always did when he talked about Mom. They heard him swallow. Ryan still remembered his mother's funeral. Dad had looked so awful they thought he might die, too.

"Without considering her own future, your aunt took six months' leave and came to help me look after you two."

The boys nodded. They'd heard all this before.

"Then, at the end of that time, I couldn't find anyone I could trust to take care of you, so she resigned from her job and offered to stay for as long as we needed her. I was selfish enough to let her."

Ryan shifted his weight from one foot to the other. His glance met Greg's. They looked away again and stared at the floor. Dad waited until he had their full attention. Then he went on.

"Two years ago, when you didn't need her quite so much, Aunt Beth began doing part-time work. She took a course at the community college, too. D'you remember?"

Both boys nodded again.

"That was to help her go back to work full time." He paused. "Then there was your accident, Greg. Beth's always blamed herself for that..."

"But it wasn't her fault!" Greg objected. "It was the dog!"

"And if you'd been wearing a helmet, you might have gotten off more lightly," Dad said. "I still don't know why you weren't."

"Neither do I." Greg shook his head. "I don't remember anything about it."

"I didn't mean to get into that," said Dad. "I only wanted to point out all the sacrifices your aunt has made for us. Even now, you'd still be in the hospital, Greg, if it wasn't for Beth. They only let you come home because she'd been a nurse, and they thought she could give you as much help as they could..."

Ryan wasn't so sure about that.

"So I don't want you to worry her. Now, you'd better come out and apologize, and eat your dinner."

"We've already said we were sorry," Greg grumbled.

"You didn't sound very sorry," said Dad.

"Wait a minute, Dad." Ryan stopped him. "We don't want to upset Aunt Beth, but she's making some pretty impossible rules around here."

"Like wanting you to be home on time?"

Ryan shook his head. "I don't mean that," he said. "It's more that she doesn't want Greg to go anywhere without her. Especially with me."

"Beth did say something about that. She's concerned that you're not making as much progress with your walking as you should, Greg. And she feels your attitude isn't helping, Ryan."

"That's not true, Dad!" Greg's cheeks flushed red with anger.

"You might not agree," said Dad, "but your aunt is better qualified than any of us to decide about that." He made for the door. "Come on. Dinner's ready."

Greg sighed and pushed on the wheels of his chair. Ryan followed him out into the kitchen.

Chapter 8

Aunt Beth carried plates of food to the table. Her face was pale, almost gray. Wispy hair had escaped from its clasp and strayed across one cheek. Her mouth drooped at the corners.

How can she be that upset just because we were late coming home, Ryan wondered, as he helped Greg maneuver his chair up to the table.

"Sorry we didn't get home on time, Aunt Beth," he said.

"Me, too," said Greg.

"We'll say no more about it, then," said Aunt Beth, "as long as it doesn't happen again." She put the plates on the table. "And I don't want you to go out without me, Greg," she added.

Greg took an angry breath.

Dad interrupted him before he could argue. "Just a minute, Greg," he said, and turned to his sister.

"Do you think that's necessary, Beth? I'm sure Greg will be quite safe with Ryan."

"I don't think he is safe," Aunt Beth said. "Look what happened today."

"Nothing happened today – except that we had a lot of fun," said Ryan.

"Well," said Greg, pushing away his plate, "if I can't go back to the beach, at least I've got a souvenir." He reached under his blanket and dragged something out. "Trixie's stick!" He slapped it down on the table.

That did cause an uproar! Grains of sand scattered over the table. Aunt Beth dropped her fork and picked up the stick between her thumb and one finger. She held it as though it was something disgusting.

"This has been chewed by a dog!" she declared.

"Yes," agreed Greg. "By Trixie."

Aunt Beth tossed the stick into the garbage and glared at Ryan.

"After all that happened to Gregory because of a dog, you had to take him out where all those dogs are?"

"It wasn't all," Ryan said quietly. "Trixie is one very small dog. We threw sticks for her on the beach. That's all."

"And she rode home on my knee," added Greg defiantly.

Aunt Beth washed her hands at the sink and picked

up her plate. "It's a pity you've never worked in a hospital," she said. "If you'd seen some of the dreadful dog bites inflicted on innocent children that I've seen, you'd never want to go near another one!" She strode past them toward the hallway. "I'll finish my meal in my room!" she announced over her shoulder.

The door banged shut behind her.

Greg glided over to the garbage and rescued Trixie's stick.

"That wasn't much of an apology, was it?" said Dad.

Both boys looked at each other, at the table, everywhere except at their father.

"I don't see why you can't do as your aunt wants," he went on. "You must realize we can't go on with these continual arguments."

"Look, Dad," Ryan said, "we'll be thirteen next month. I've got a responsible job at the kennels. Greg would have a job, too, if it wasn't for..." He waved his hand at Greg's chair. "Aunt Beth shouldn't panic if we're a few minutes late. We didn't mean to be. We wouldn't have been if it wasn't for the dogcatcher."

"The dogcatcher?"

"Yes – he caught us with Trixie on the people's beach instead of the dogs' beach."

"You mean he *nearly* caught us." Greg grinned, remembering the man puzzling over their tracks. "He would have, if I hadn't hidden Trixie under my blanket."

Ryan saw a sparkle in his brother's eyes that he hadn't seen for ages. Dad saw it, too. "But why didn't you take her to the dogs' beach? You know the rules," he said.

"Rachel and I couldn't push Greg on the soft sand," explained Ryan.

"So you see, it's mostly my fault," interrupted Greg, "but Aunt Beth keeps on blaming Ryan."

Dad frowned and shook his head. He was completely confused by this time. "How about you start from the beginning," he suggested, "and tell me the whole story."

Between them, they explained how Trixie came to be at the kennels and how her owner had died. They told him about Rachel helping get Greg out to go to obedience school, how clever Trixie was. They told him everything – except about the puppies.

"And you're paying for Trixie out of the money you earn at the kennels?" Dad asked.

Ryan nodded. "If I don't, Mr. Stein will send her to the animal shelter. You know what that means."

Dad looked at Greg. "I thought you didn't like dogs," he said.

Greg squirmed in his wheelchair. He didn't like admitting he'd changed his mind. "Trixie's not like other dogs, Dad. She's just so smart. You wouldn't believe how fast she learns things."

"Mmmm," said Dad. "I can see you're convinced, anyway. I suppose I'll have to convince Aunt Beth now."

Hurrah, thought Ryan. We've talked him into it.

"Can Trixie live here with us?" Greg asked.

"That's going too far. Let's try one step at a time. What do you want most?"

"A ramp so we don't have to struggle up and down those steps," Ryan said promptly.

"All right," said Dad. "That would help Aunt Beth, as well. You get going on the dishes, Ryan. I'll find someone to build the ramp." He picked up the phone book.

"I'll help with the dishes," Greg insisted. He took a tray from the cupboard and piled the dirty plates on it. He used one hand to steady it on his knees, the other to propel his chair over to the sink.

When the dishes were dry, he used the tray to ferry them to the cupboard. Ryan helped him put them away.

Greg enjoyed doing that, Ryan thought, as he wiped the counter. Fancy anyone enjoying doing the dishes! I spend most of my life trying to avoid them. Maybe if I'd been like Greg, and *couldn't* do them... That's not right. It wasn't that Greg couldn't do them. We just didn't expect him to.

Ryan bent down to put away the dish rack and detergent. Greg fed Zip and went to his room. The kitchen was silent. Ryan looked up.

Aunt Beth stood in the doorway.

Chapter 9

"You finally got your way," she said, "about the ramp." She scraped the remainder of her meal – most of it, Ryan thought – into the garbage can. She put her plate in the sink and rinsed it.

Ryan didn't know what to say. He couldn't say he was sorry about the ramp, because he wasn't. He couldn't say he was glad, either. That would have caused more trouble. So he said nothing. Aunt Beth's back was bent and her shoulders slumped. Even without seeing her face he knew how she felt.

Pictures ran through his mind of Aunt Beth as she used to be. Of her taking them to school sports days, baking two birthday cakes so both twins would feel special, making a game of hiding their presents until Christmas morning, laughing and cheering him on to win his races at swimming club. This wasn't the same Aunt Beth. That one had disappeared when Greg got hurt.

"Aunt Beth?" Ryan whispered, and stood beside her. He had to say something – but what? She turned around. He saw frustration and despair. She dried her plate, knife, and fork, and put them away. Suddenly she straightened up.

"If you want to take over looking after Gregory," she said sharply, "make sure you do it properly," and she left the room.

All right, thought Ryan angrily, I will!

—————

The next day, before Ryan and Dad left for work, three men came to start the ramp. By evening, the only thing left to do was the handrail. Greg told Ryan all the details. He'd watched the buzz of every saw cut and the whang of every nail.

"They've put netting on the ramp so no one will slip if it's raining," he explained.

"We'll be able to use it tomorrow night when we go to obedience school," said Ryan. "I can take you up and down easily."

"I'll take *myself* up and down!" said Greg. "It's not too steep." Then he looked behind him, down the empty hall. "Come in here. I want to tell you something."

Ryan followed Greg into his bedroom. He picked

Zip up off Greg's bed and held her under his chin. Zip purred.

"Shut the door," Greg said quietly. Ryan gave it a push with his foot. "It's Aunt Beth. Usually she's chasing after me, saying, 'D'you want this?' or, 'D'you want that?' But today I've hardly seen her."

"What about lunchtime? She was here then."

"Yes, but she didn't say much, did she? Just fixed lunch, you remember, and went away to her room. She went to the grocery store, then she spent most of the afternoon in her room, too. If I called her, she'd come, but she hasn't even nagged me to do my exercises."

Ryan remembered Aunt Beth saying he had to look after Greg properly. Maybe he should start now. The exercises were important if Greg was going to walk again, but it was no good telling him he had to do them. Ryan would have to be a bit cunning.

"What kind of exercises?" Ryan asked.

"To make my leg muscles and my joints strong. Look, I'll show you," Greg answered. He maneuvered himself onto his bed and leaned against the wall.

"The first one's for ankles," he said and rotated his feet several times to the left, then to the right. He continued on with exercises for the lower leg, the knee, and the thigh.

"You're pretty good at those," said Ryan. "What d'you do next?"

"I'm supposed to walk, hanging onto the bars." He pointed to the set of bars near the far wall. Ryan had always thought they looked like the parallel bars at the gym.

"How d'you do that?" Ryan asked.

"They showed me in the hospital. You put your arms over each side and walk along in between."

"Come on, then." Ryan sounded more confident than he felt. But Greg wasn't going to be tricked into doing any more. He shook his head. "I'm not ready yet. Aunt Beth and I argue about that every day. She says I'm ready, but I know I'm not!"

"What does the doctor say?"

Greg glared at the floor. He didn't answer.

"What does he say?" Ryan insisted.

Greg stuck his chin out defiantly. "He says I'm ready. But what does he know?"

———

Greg often hung around in his bathrobe and slippers, refusing to get dressed. But when Ryan arrived home for lunch the next day, he was ready to go out.

"Where are you going?" asked Ryan as he sat down at the table.

"With you," Greg answered, his mouth filled with peanut butter sandwich.

Aunt Beth poured some coffee and continued eating. She said nothing. When lunch was finished, she went off to her room. A few minutes later, Greg hooked a bag over his armrest and wheeled himself down the hall. He put his head in at her door. "We're off now, Aunt Beth. Be back at dinnertime."

"What did she say?" Ryan asked, as he wheeled Greg down the new ramp.

"Nothing. Didn't take much notice. Just nodded her head. She has books spread all over her table. I think she's taking notes from them."

"What d'you want to come to the kennels for?" asked Ryan, changing the subject.

"You'll see," Greg smirked.

"You'd better keep out of the way," warned Ryan. "Rachel's dad can get pretty crabby."

When they got to the kennels, Ryan took Greg up to the house. Greg asked Ryan to bring Trixie in to him. The little dog bounded up onto Greg's knee and washed his face with her tongue.

"Sit!" he said, holding her with both hands. When she settled down, he dragged an old hairbrush and a comb with strong, wide teeth out of his bag. He combed all the

loose, rough hairs from her coat. It took more than an hour. Then he used the brush. When he'd finished, her coat was a silky curtain. Her tail, a feathery flag, waved behind her as she pranced around his chair.

"How's that?" Greg called to Ryan, as he brushed the brown hairs from his clothes. "We'll have the best-looking dog at the school."

"Just great!" Ryan said admiringly, but in his mind he saw the handsome German shepherd. He knew the big dog was disobedient – but whose fault was it? Rachel said he was a stupid dog, and no one could ever do anything with him. Not true, thought Ryan. If I had him, I'd soon train him. He imagined the dog walking beside him onto the platform to accept the cup for most points at the trials. He saw himself racing along the beach, rolling and tumbling on the sand with the big dog – just having fun!

"Trixie, come!" Greg's voice roused him from his dream. The little dog trotted up to Greg and sat, waiting for the next command. She certainly was a smart little dog.

"You'll do well tonight, won't you, Trix?" Greg bent forward and stroked her ears.

But Trixie had been to her last lesson.

"I've just got time for my exercises before dinner," Greg said, as Ryan pushed him up the ramp. Great, thought Ryan. No one had to hassle him.

Aunt Beth was in her room. The books that had been spread everywhere before were stacked in a neat pile.

"I'm going next door to see Mrs. Cooper for a minute," she said. "Will you set the table for me please, Ryan?"

The evening meal was a quiet one. Dad had called earlier to say he was working late. Aunt Beth spoke only to say "yes" or "no" to the boys' questions. After the first two, there weren't many.

Ryan was putting the dishes away when the phone rang.

"I'll get it!" shouted Greg from the bathroom.

Ryan couldn't hear what Greg said, but he knew

something exciting had happened.

"Who is it?" Ryan asked, poking his head around the corner. Greg put the phone down.

"It was Rachel."

"What did she want?"

"Bet you can't guess," he teased. Before Ryan had time to guess, he said, "It's about Trixie."

"She's had her puppies?"

Greg nodded.

"How many?"

Greg laughed. "One!"

"One? Bet she'll have more. I'm going to see."

"Hang on. I'm coming, too!"

"Better tell Aunt Beth," warned Ryan. "I don't think she'll be pleased, though. You know how she gets upset about anything to do with dogs."

"I don't care. I'm going."

Chapter 10

Ryan was right. Aunt Beth wasn't pleased about Greg going out again, and it annoyed her that they didn't explain where they were going and why. She'd have been more annoyed if they had! As they disappeared down the road she watched out the window.

"Hope we don't hit a rock," said Greg, as the wheelchair hurtled along the sidewalk.

Rachel was waiting for them at the gate. She swung it open as they turned in.

"Where is she?" Greg demanded.

"How many puppies now?" Ryan wanted to know.

"In her cage, and still only one," Rachel replied. "Dad's not very pleased with us for keeping quiet about it, either. He says we'll be overrun by a horde of mongrels."

"Let's see," insisted Greg. But when they reached the path leading to the cages, it was too narrow for the wheelchair. "Rats!" he said.

"There's only one thing to do," said Ryan. "You'll have to walk. It's not far." He pointed to a cage about three yards away.

"Don't be stupid!" Greg grumbled. "It might as well be on the other side of town!"

"I don't mean by yourself," said Ryan. "Rachel and I'll get on each side. You can put your arms around our necks, and we'll join hands behind you."

Greg looked doubtful.

"First, let's move that bench, Rachel. We'll put it by the cage for Greg to sit on," Ryan went on. They took an end each of the long bench and scraped it across the cement until it was opposite Trixie's cage.

"Now," he said, and put one arm behind Greg's back. Rachel did the same on the other side. They grabbed one of Greg's arms each. Before he could argue, they swung them around their necks and stood up. Although Greg didn't take much of his own weight, he stood up, too. He had to!

"Left! Right!" ordered Ryan. Slowly Greg moved one foot, then the other. Ryan felt Greg's fingers dig into his shoulder, and he had a horrible thought. What if he wasn't ready to walk? What if the doctor was wrong? Maybe Greg should have gone on with the exercises for a few more days. All this to get a look at Trixie's puppy! Was it worth it?

At last. The bench. Ryan and Rachel lowered Greg slowly onto it.

"All right?" asked Rachel.

Greg nodded, but Ryan saw the sweat soaking through his brother's shirt and the dampness on his forehead. It hadn't been easy.

"Can't see much," complained Greg, looking into the darkness of the sleeping compartment. "Looks like it was a lot of trouble for nothing."

"Just a minute," said Rachel. She went into the cage and lifted the lid of Trixie's box. Trixie raised her head and thumped her tail against the back wall.

"She's pleased to see us," said Ryan.

The puppy was small and dark brown – darker than Trixie. He lay very still, cuddled up against her.

"Do you want to hold him?" Rachel asked Greg.

"Won't she mind?"

"I don't think so, Trixie trusts us. I'll put him back if she objects."

Rachel scooped up the little creature in both hands and carried him out to Greg. Trixie followed. She pushed in between the two boys and wagged her tail. She didn't worry at all until her puppy squeaked. Then she stood on her hind legs and nuzzled him.

"My turn," said Ryan. He took the puppy. Both eyes

were shut tight, and his ears seemed stuck to the sides of his head. His nose was blunt, not pointed yet, like his mother's. Ryan stroked his damp coat with one finger.

"Do you think he'll have long hair like Trixie?" said Greg.

"Hard to tell," said Rachel. "But it's long around the back of his neck. Look!" She lifted a few fine strands between two fingers. "Better put him back now," she said, and she lifted the puppy off Ryan's lap.

"Will she have any more?" asked Greg.

"Doesn't look like it."

"They usually have more than one, don't they?"

"Yes," said Rachel, as she shut the cage door with Trixie and her puppy inside. "At least three or four. Sometimes as many as ten or eleven."

The outside gate clanged, and Mr. Stein came down the path.

"Is this what you call double trouble?" he asked. He sounded cross, but the corners of his mouth twitched up into a grin.

They were all too excited about the puppy to care what Mr. Stein said. They sat around for awhile, talking. Rachel and Greg argued about what to call him.

"We'll have to choose a boy's name," said Rachel.

"Let's call him Rex," said Greg. "It means king."

"He might not look like a king, though," said Rachel.

"Wait until he's a bit older," suggested Ryan. "You'll be able to see what suits him then." As long as they don't want to call him Ringo, he thought. I'm saving that for my dog – when I get one.

Chapter 11

When they got home, Greg tried getting up and down the ramp on his own. Down wasn't too bad. He used the brake to keep himself from going too fast. But going up was harder. He wished he had an electric chair like the man at the dog school. At last he managed it by pulling himself up on the handrail a little way, then putting on the brake to rest before going a bit farther. Ryan wanted to help, but Greg wouldn't let him.

"Go and play on the computer or feed Zip or something," he said.

When Ryan went inside, Dad and Aunt Beth were in the kitchen talking about something private. Something they didn't want him to hear. He could tell by the way they stopped suddenly when he went in. Then they went on about what a great day it had been. He'd been going to tell them about Greg on the ramp, but if they had secrets from him, he wouldn't bother. Anyway, if they found out what Greg was doing, they'd try to stop him. What trouble he'd cause then!

Ryan drifted off to the sunroom. He could see the ramp from the window. There he could keep an eye on Greg.

When he looked out, Greg was flushed and panting, but he was at the top. Ryan gave him the "thumbs up" sign. Greg grinned and pointed to the door handle. It was too high to reach from the wheelchair. It hadn't mattered before, because even if he'd got the door open from the inside, there was nowhere to go. Nowhere, except down a flight of steep steps.

Ryan opened the door. Greg wheeled himself in. Ryan put out a hand to stop him as he made for the kitchen.

"Don't go down there," he said quietly. "Dad and Aunt Beth are having a private talk."

"What about?"

"Don't know. They stopped when I went in." Ryan hesitated. Now that Greg had won a battle with the ramp, was this the time to try the next step?

"Let's go to your room," he suggested, "and see if you can walk holding onto the bars."

Greg gave the floor a stony stare. "I can't."

"You haven't tried. You walked with Rachel and me helping you."

"But I can't reach up to the bars."

"I'll help you up."

Reluctantly, Greg turned his chair and wheeled himself into his room. He stopped just inside the door. Ryan could see he didn't want to go any farther, but he pushed the wheelchair across the room, anyway, and stopped with Greg facing the ends of the bars.

"Put on the brake," he said.

Greg's shaky hand pulled back the lever.

"What are you nervous about?" Ryan asked.

"I'm not just nervous. I'm scared! I tried to do this once with Aunt Beth. She was scared, too. She knew I couldn't do it."

"That's dumb! What was she scared about?"

"Don't know... but I saw the panic in her face. And when she started to lift me, her arms shook. She put me down again in a hurry and said it was my fault because I didn't try." Greg was almost crying.

"But you walked with Rachel and me helping," Ryan said. Greg looked down at his hands. They twisted and clenched in his lap. His fingers turned white.

"Just one try," Ryan insisted. "I'll stand behind you and lift you up. When I lift, you put your arms over the rails and try to take your weight."

"What if I can't?"

"I'll put you down again. That's all." Ryan made himself sound calm and confident. He didn't really feel it.

Before Greg could think of any more arguments, Ryan bent his knees and put his hands under his brother's arms. With his feet apart to steady himself, he straightened up and lifted. "Now, get your arms over the bars."

Greg's hands scrambled at the bars until his elbows rested along the top. Ryan felt his brother's heart thumping. He'd expected Greg to be light because he was so thin – and he was, too. But had he grown! He was two inches taller than Ryan.

"Not being able to walk hasn't stopped you growing," he joked. Greg gave a tiny grin. Ryan felt him relax a little. "Do you want me to let go now?"

"Not yet." Greg's muscles tensed again.

"All right. I can hang on as long as you like," Ryan lied. It wasn't Greg's weight. It was more the awkward hold. The bars prevented him from standing up straight. He had to keep his knees bent.

Ryan held him there as long as he could. At last he said, "Do you want me to put you down, or let you go?"

"Put me down." Greg let go of the bars, and Ryan slowly lowered him into the chair.

Ryan stood up and straightened his back. Greg

looked pale. He was damp with sweat.

"You all right?" Ryan asked anxiously. Greg nodded. He gave a shaky grin.

"It wasn't too bad," he said.

Ryan leaned on the bars. "No, it wasn't too bad, was it?" They grinned at each other.

Behind his grin, Ryan still wondered if he was doing the right thing.

Chapter 12

"I'm going to the kennels after breakfast," Greg said as he was eating cereal the next morning.

"What's at the kennels?" asked Dad.

Greg and Ryan didn't want to talk about Trixie in front of Aunt Beth. They'd both agreed not to.

"I want to watch Ryan working," Greg said. "It's a sight not often seen."

Ryan reached over and pretended to cuff Greg's ear.

"How about helping Aunt Beth with the dishes. You can go with Ryan at lunchtime," Dad suggested. "Your bedroom could do with a good cleanup, too."

"OK," said Greg. "I'll do the dishes and my room and take myself to the kennels when I've finished."

"I don't think you should go alone." Aunt Beth's face had a worried frown. Greg looked surprised. This was the first time since their argument that she'd tried to stop him from doing anything.

"I can get up and down the ramp now," he said, "and crossing the street's no trouble. I'll come home with Ryan at lunchtime." Aunt Beth looked up at Dad. He shrugged his shoulders. She finished her breakfast in silence.

Ryan set off for work shortly after. Only four dogs needed exercising that morning. Most had gone home the night before, and the incoming bunch weren't expected until late afternoon. When he'd finished that job, he called to Trixie.

She left her sleeping puppy and had a drink and some of the biscuits Ryan put in her bowl. Then she followed him around to the front of the building. The cat food had been delivered to the gate. It was Ryan's job to stow it in the fridge.

As he picked up the first box, he saw Greg speeding along the sidewalk toward the kennels.

"Hi," Ryan called. "Your friend's waiting for you!" He pointed down at Trixie.

"Open the gate," Greg said. "I can't reach the catch."

Ryan flicked the catch over and swung the gate open. A noisy, old car rumbled around the corner and headed toward them. As it passed the gate, Trixie shot out from behind Ryan and raced after it.

"Trixie!" Ryan shouted. "Come here!" He looked around, afraid that Mr. Stein might be watching.

Greg laughed. "That one's so slow she might catch it!"

Then something happened that they would never forget. A dark green motorcycle roared down the road. They hadn't heard it before because of the noisy car.

Trixie turned to obey Ryan's call. She was in the middle of the road when the bike roared past. They didn't see it hit her, but when it had gone, she lay in the gutter.

Ryan picked her up. There was no blood on her. No marks. But he knew she was dead. She lay in his arms, limp like his old teddy bear. He carried her over to the sidewalk where Greg waited, white-faced beneath his blond hair. He put out one trembling hand to touch her silky coat.

"Poor little thing," Greg whispered. "How'd it happen?"

Ryan had no answer.

Rachel bustled around the corner of the building. "I heard you calling Trixie," she said. "Was she chasing..." She stopped. "How bad?" She came closer. "Is she dead?"

Ryan nodded. Rachel took her from him and held her for a few moments. Then they carried her out to a grassy patch beneath a tree at the back of the kennels. It was where the Stein family buried their pets when they died. Rachel laid the little dog on the ground.

Greg watched while the other two took turns digging a hole. When it was deep enough Rachel leaned her shovel against the tree and pushed her hair back. Her eyes were sad and her mouth drooped at the corners.

"I'll get something to wrap her in," she said.

Ryan couldn't keep his eyes off the dog lying still on the grass. Only a few minutes ago she'd leaped around, delighted to be with him.

The breeze stirred the fine hairs of her well-groomed coat. It had taken Greg ages to get it looking so beautiful. In a few weeks she could have left the pup for long enough to go back to obedience school. She was so smart and obedient, she'd soon have made up the lessons she missed. It was being obedient that killed her. If she hadn't run back across the road when Ryan called, she would still be alive.

Rachel came back with a large, white bag over one arm and the puppy cuddled up in the other. She laid him on Greg's lap.

"You hold him," she said. Greg cradled the puppy in his hands. It whimpered, turning its head from side to side. The tiny claws scratched at Greg's fingers.

"What's wrong with him?" he asked.

"He's hungry and he wants his mother," Ryan said crossly. He was angry with himself for not being more careful. He was so angry, he didn't feel like being patient with Greg. As he placed the bag with Trixie inside into the hole, he had a horrible, empty feeling.

"It's my fault," he said. "I shouldn't have opened the gate. And if I hadn't called her, she wouldn't have been on the road." He sniffed and wiped his sweater sleeve across his nose.

Greg cuddled the puppy against himself. "No. It's my fault," he said. "If I hadn't insisted on coming here this morning, the gate would have been shut."

"It's nobody's fault." Mr. Stein strode along the path from the house. "Trixie was a cute little dog, but she chased cars. That's why it happened."

"She was a smart little dog, Dad," Rachel said. "We could have taught her not to."

"I don't know how," said Mr. Stein. "I've never cured a car-chasing dog yet."

He watched them fill in the hole with the rest of the earth. "And what are you going to do about that?" He pointed to the puppy.

Rachel, Ryan, and Greg looked at him, and then at each other.

"I've got a book on rearing orphan puppies somewhere," Mr. Stein said grudgingly. "Come with me and I'll give it to you." He took a few steps toward the house, then stopped. "He looks hungry. You'll have to feed him right away."

Mr. Stein took them inside. "Beat up an egg yolk in a cup of milk," he said. "That will do until you can buy some lamb's milk. It's good for puppies. Warm a tablespoon of the mixture – lukewarm, that's all – and feed it to him with this." He gave Ryan a plastic eyedropper. "Keep the rest in the fridge until you need it. Germs grow in stale milk, so you'll have to clean everything you use really well. If you don't, he'll get sick. He could die."

Rachel rummaged through the cupboards to find the right-sized bowl and the beater. Greg still cuddled the puppy. It had been quiet for awhile, but now it whimpered and snuffled around his hands again. Ryan watched. He felt helpless and angry. How were they going to care for such a tiny creature? He imagined finding it cold and dead, like its mother, because they hadn't known exactly what to do.

"It's hard to get such a little bit of milk just warm," complained Rachel. "If we get it too hot, the egg will get lumpy." At last she decided to make the pan hot with boiling water, tip the water out, and put the milk in the hot pan. She dipped her finger in. "That's just right," she said. She put the open end of the eyedropper into the warm milk, squeezed the rubber knob at the other end, then slowly released it. The milk sucked up into the eyedropper. "Now," she said, "how do we get him to drink it?"

"Let me do it," said Ryan. He sat beside Greg and lifted the puppy's head with one hand. He slid the eyedropper into the corner of its mouth and gave it a gentle squeeze. The whimpering stopped. He felt the puppy's throat move.

"He swallowed."

Ryan squeezed again. Again the puppy swallowed. Ryan kept squeezing until all the milk was gone. The puppy made a few faint grunting noises, wriggled around until he was comfortable in Greg's hands, and slept.

For a moment Ryan felt a flicker of hope. Maybe the puppy would live. But then, for a moment he thought, what's the point? Who would want it?

Then Greg said, "Now what?"

Ryan and Rachel looked at each other.

They didn't know.

Chapter 13

"There's a chapter on raising dogs by hand in this book," said Mr. Stein. Ryan reached out to take it. "But I don't want you spending all your time fooling around with that pup. You're paid to work for me, remember." He tried to look stern. "I don't expect you'll have much luck, anyway. I've never seen anyone hand rear anything so small." He bent over and touched the fine hair on the puppy's head. It opened its mouth and yawned. They all grinned. Even Mr. Stein.

Ryan turned to the book. He flicked through the pages until he came to the chapter he wanted.

"Here's what we need," he announced a few moments later. "A small box..."

"A very small box," Greg interrupted.

"A hot-water bottle, some old cloths, newspaper, and some paper towels."

"We've got everything here except the hot-water

bottle," said Rachel.

"We have one at home," said Ryan.

"You mean Aunt Beth has one," warned Greg.

"Same thing," said Ryan. He looked at his watch. "Nearly lunchtime. I'll bring it back at one o'clock. Can you keep him in a warm place until then, Rachel?"

They lined a box with newspaper. "That's to keep out the draft," said Ryan. Then they made a nest with the cloth and covered it with paper towels.

"Why d'you need paper towels?" asked Greg.

"If he was a real baby, we'd use diapers," grinned Rachel. "This way we change the paper towels instead."

Greg blushed. "I hadn't thought of that," he said.

They put the puppy in his box in a sunny corner of Trixie's old cage.

"He'll be all right there until after lunch," said Rachel. She stood there with Ryan for a moment. They stared sadly in at the box, remembering the missing dog.

"We need a marker to show where she's buried," said Ryan on the way home.

"I'll make one," said Greg.

"What will you make it from?"

"I have something. You'll see."

When they got home, Greg insisted on getting himself up the ramp. It was easier this time. Ryan opened the door and they went in. Zip ran out of Greg's bedroom, purring and meowing.

"Gregory?" Aunt Beth called him from the kitchen.

Greg went to find out what she wanted. Zip rode on his knee.

Ryan slipped into the bathroom and searched in the cupboard for the hot-water bottle.

"She won't miss it," he muttered. "Not in the summertime." He took it back to his room and put it on his bed. Before he went to the kitchen, he covered it with his jacket. He didn't want another argument with Aunt Beth. It had been a horrible day already. There was no need to make it worse!

Greg sat at the table, glowering.

"What's wrong?" Ryan asked. Greg glared at his sandwich, but he didn't answer.

"He has a doctor's appointment this afternoon," Aunt Beth said. She brought Ryan's plate to the table.

"I don't need to go to the doctor!" Greg snapped. "He doesn't know what he's talking about."

"Of course, you have to go," Ryan said soothingly. He picked up a sandwich.

"But I have to go back to the kennels. What about Trixie's..." Ryan's warning stare stopped him before he said any more. It wouldn't help for Aunt Beth to know about the puppy.

"I might have known that dog was at the bottom of this. I told your father he should have put a stop to that nonsense!" Aunt Beth's mouth snapped shut.

Greg looked up at her. His eyes swam with tears. He rubbed them with the back of his hand.

"You'll be glad to hear you won't have to worry about her any more," he muttered, and wheeled himself away from the table. Then he stopped suddenly at the door and swung around, almost shouting. "Because she's dead. Trixie's dead!"

Aunt Beth started to follow him down the hall. Then she turned to Ryan.

"What happened?" she asked.

Ryan sat with the sandwich frozen midway between the plate and his mouth. He put it down and explained about the motorcycle. Then he said, "Mr. Stein wasn't surprised she'd been run over. He said we'd never be able to stop her from chasing things. Greg thinks we could have trained her not to, but I don't know... The trouble is, he blames himself. He thinks if he hadn't come to the kennels this morning she wouldn't have been on the road."

Ryan picked at the remainder of his sandwich, then pushed the plate away. He didn't want to talk about Trixie anymore. Not to Aunt Beth. "I'm going back to work now. Tell Greg I'll see him tonight."

Greg's door was shut. Zip waited patiently outside. Ryan hesitated. He had a few minutes to spare, and Greg needed something to take his mind off Trixie. He opened the door, stepped inside, and shut it quietly.

"We'll have another try before I go," Ryan said, nodding toward the bars. Reluctantly, Greg wheeled himself to the starting point. Ryan helped him up.

"Hold on," he said. "I'm letting go this time."

Greg hooked his arms over the bars and took two quick breaths. "OK," he said, and Ryan slowly lowered his arms. A nervous grin flickered across Greg's face. One foot moved forward, then the other. He slid both arms along the bars and rested for a moment. He went through the whole routine several times. At last he reached the end.

"You were great!" said Ryan, and he helped Greg back into the wheelchair.

"I wasn't too bad, was I?" Greg said, rubbing his face with his sleeve to wipe away the sweat.

Ryan looked at his watch. "You were good, all right! But I'm really late now! We'll try again tonight. And you'd better not tell Aunt Beth I've been helping you."

On the way out, Ryan picked up his jacket from his bed. He made sure the hot-water bottle was tucked inside it.

Rachel took the hot-water bottle from Ryan and filled it with warm water. She put it on top of the newspaper and tucked the cloths around it. She covered them with some clean paper towels.

"In you go." She lowered the puppy into his warm nest. He squeaked a few times and settled himself to sleep. "He'll have to go in the feed shed. Dad's put another dog in Trixie's old cage," Rachel said. Ryan held the box, while Rachel moved some bags of dog biscuits to make room.

The puppy's eyes were still two dark lines. They wouldn't open for another nine days. His ears were tiny flaps close to his head. Ryan watched his sides go up and down with each breath. Once he gave a little shudder and squeaked. Then he relaxed back into sleep. Ryan wondered if he'd been dreaming.

In between doing the chores, Ryan and Rachel took turns looking into the shed. If the puppy was restless or whining, they fed him an eyedropper-full of milk.

"It looks like he'll need feeding at least every two or three hours," said Ryan at his afternoon break. "And the book says it's a good idea to groom a puppy with a warm, damp cloth or some cotton. That's instead of the mother licking him."

"Let's see," said Rachel, taking the book. But before

she had a chance to read about it, her mother called her.

"Rachel! Come inside, will you!"

"Coming!" Rachel called back. "I wonder what she wants," Rachel said to Ryan. "She usually likes to get me *out* of the house at this time of day." She handed the book back and disappeared inside.

Ryan filled the hot-water bottle again, settled the pup down, and took the first dog out for its exercise. This was the part of the day he enjoyed most. Today, though, his mind was more on the box in the shed. As he returned each dog to its cage and before he got the next one, he looked in through the window to make sure all was well.

Ryan took a break at four-thirty to feed and groom the puppy. That made him late finishing. Rachel still hadn't come back. Mr. Stein had disappeared, too.

When Rachel finally reappeared she looked worried.

"I've got to go and stay with Aunt Celia," she said. "She's got this new baby. Mom promised I'd help her with the other two kids for a couple of weeks. I'd forgotten all about it."

"What about the puppy?" Ryan could imagine all sorts of complications if Rachel wasn't there to look after him at night.

Rachel shrugged her shoulders.

"I'll come back as soon as I can, but you and Greg can manage between you," she said, and she ran back into the house.

Ryan hoped she was right. In the meantime he'd have to take the puppy with him everywhere he went. He'd have to be its mother!

He covered the box with his jacket to keep out the cold air, then he tucked it under his arm and set off toward home. At the convenience store he bought some cotton and paper towels. Farther along the road was the vet. Ryan went there for the powdered lamb's milk.

What could he say to Aunt Beth? If only he could persuade her to let him keep the puppy at home, he'd soon talk Dad around. But there was no chance of that. He'd just have to make certain she didn't find out.

And what would Zip think about having a puppy in the house?

Chapter 14

Now that Rachel had gone away, it was just as well Greg had changed his mind about dogs. He could help look after the pup. Maybe it would work out all right, after all.

The house was empty when Ryan got home. He filled the hot-water bottle again, fed and groomed the puppy, and put the box in the corner of his room. Zip meowed at the window. Ryan let her in. The kitten sniffed around the box and stared in at the puppy. Her orange fur stood on end and she arched her back.

Ryan laughed at her. "Silly cat," he said, as he cuddled the prickly kitten. Just then the van stopped at the gate. Ryan carried Zip out to meet Greg. He was careful to shut his door. Aunt Beth would be tired after driving Greg around all afternoon. This was no time to introduce her to a puppy. Not one that was sleeping on her hot-water bottle.

Aunt Beth walked up the sidewalk alone. The back of the van was empty.

"Where's Greg?"

"In the hospital."

Something jolted inside Ryan. What had happened? Not another accident? Then he panicked. Had he done some damage trying to get Greg to walk? "What's wrong?"

"It's nothing new," Aunt Beth said, as she went into her bedroom and took off her jacket. "Just that when I told the doctor Gregory still hasn't started walking, he said he couldn't understand why..."

"But..." Ryan began to interrupt, then stopped. Aunt Beth wouldn't be pleased to find out he'd been helping Greg behind her back.

"So he's doing more X rays and some other tests. Gregory will be in there for a day or two, that's all."

Aunt Beth sounded unconcerned as she bustled around the kitchen preparing dinner, but Ryan knew she was worried. Maybe things were even more serious than she said.

Aunt Beth was watching TV in the living room and Dad was mowing the lawn. Ryan mixed up the lamb's milk and put it in a jar. He hoped the sound of the mower disguised the noise he made with the beater. He washed the eyedropper, filled it with the warm milk, and hid the jar at the back of the refrigerator.

Suddenly, the TV noise went off and Aunt Beth called to him as he passed the living room door. "Is that Zip I can hear, Ryan? What's wrong with her?"

"I'll have a look," said Ryan. He didn't stop, because she might see what was in his hand, and he already knew what had made the noise.

This time one fill of the eyedropper wasn't enough for the hungry puppy. He still snuffled around looking for more. Ryan unbuttoned his shirt and tucked the pup inside. Maybe he'd keep quiet if he was cuddled up against something warm and alive – at least for as long as it took Ryan to get a refill.

Music came from the TV again as Ryan headed back to the kitchen, but the mower had stopped. Dad came in while Ryan was putting warm milk into the eyedropper. He stared for a minute, but he was used to Ryan fiddling around in the kitchen.

"I won't ask what you're doing," he said. "Just see that you clean up after yourself and don't leave a mess for Aunt Beth." Ryan nodded. He had no intention of leaving any trace of his activities in the kitchen for Aunt Beth to find.

Seven-thirty. At last the puppy was fed, the paper towels changed, and the hot-water bottle filled. Ryan flopped back on his bed. He was exhausted. It wasn't just looking after the puppy that was such hard work. Having to keep everything a secret was a problem, too. If only he could tell Aunt Beth. But he couldn't risk her making a fuss. The way she's been lately, she was sure to!

With Rachel and Greg away, there was no one else to help. He couldn't take any chances. Ryan glanced down at the puppy. This tiny life was his responsibility alone.

Ryan's eyelids closed.

It was dark when the puppy woke him with its whimpering. He turned on the bedside lamp and picked the little thing up. Its bed was wet and the hot-water bottle was cold. Ryan was cold, too. He'd gone to sleep on top of his blankets – instead of under them.

The puppy snuggled up against him and was quiet for a moment. Before the whimpering started up again Ryan got out of bed, put the eyedropper in his pocket, and sneaked down the hall to the kitchen. He closed the kitchen door before he turned on the light. What time was it? He looked up at the clock. Eleven o'clock. Three hours since the pup's last feed. I s'pose that's about right, he thought.

Ryan warmed the milk and fed the puppy. He tucked

him inside his shirt while he refilled the hot-water bottle and put fresh paper towels in the box. It all had to be done without waking anyone. It wasn't easy!

The pup woke Ryan twice more during the night. The last time, daylight showed through the curtains. After that, Ryan kept rubbing his eyes to keep awake. It was too early to get up, but he didn't dare shut his eyes again in case he slept in. It wouldn't do for Aunt Beth to come in and wake him.

Aunt Beth watched Ryan closely during breakfast. He knew why. He'd noticed his red-rimmed eyes and pale face in the bathroom mirror.

"Do you feel all right, Ryan?" she asked.

"Yes thanks, Aunt Beth," he said. He looked down at his cereal bowl.

"Sure you're not getting a cold or something? You were in bed very early last night," she persisted.

"I'm all right," he said, and he stood up. "I'll clear the table before I go."

He put the butter away in the fridge. At the same time he took the puppy's milk out and wriggled the jar into his pocket. It was a tight squeeze.

Dad had his nose in the morning paper. He lifted his head long enough to say, "Good-bye," and went on reading.

Ryan hurried through making his bed and picking up

his room. He'd have to get out of the house before the puppy woke again. Aunt Beth would be sure to hear him. Zip stood on her hind legs and looked into the box. She sniffed at the puppy's face and purred.

"Feeling more friendly now, are you?" Ryan said to the kitten. He pushed her gently away. Then he tucked an old sweater around the pup and piled the paper towels and the milk on top.

Zip left the box and purred around his ankles. Ryan hadn't fed her. He scooped the kitten up in one hand and took her through to the kitchen.

"Will you feed Zip this morning, Aunt Beth?" he asked, leaning around the half-open door. "I'm a bit late."

Aunt Beth nodded. He saw her glance up at the clock. She knows I'm not late, he thought, but I haven't got time to worry about that now.

Chapter 15

By working as fast as he could, and feeding the puppy before work, at morning break, and before lunch, Ryan managed to fit everything in.

When he went home for lunch, he put the puppy in the feed shed. For a moment he stood watching it. He stroked its head with one finger. It sighed and snuffled, then went back to sleep. How tiny it was! But it must be growing. It was eating enough.

Dad and Ryan got home for lunch at the same time.

"Greg would like to see you this afternoon," Dad said. "I've got an appointment in town at five-thirty. I could meet you at the kennels, drop you off at the hospital, and pick you up again at six."

"That'll be great," said Ryan, although he had no idea what he would do with the puppy. Why did Rachel have to go away just now?

The afternoon was an awful scramble. Every cage was

full, and Mr. Stein had to sort out a problem with dog food deliveries. Ryan was glad when five o'clock came. At ten past, he was waiting for Dad at the gate.

"Put your bag in the trunk," Dad said.

"It's all right. I'll keep it on my knee."

"Please yourself."

The traffic was busy, and they drove in silence. Dad stopped outside the hospital steps. Ryan hopped out. He lifted his bag gently and put it over his shoulder.

"See you at six," Dad called as he drove away. Ryan raised one hand.

"What's happened about the puppy?" were Greg's first words when he saw Ryan.

"See for yourself," said Ryan. He undid the straps on the bag, lifted the puppy out, and put it in Greg's hands. It grunted and made little whimpering sounds, then went back to sleep.

"It's grown," said Greg.

"I should hope so," said Ryan. "I've fed it enough." Then he told Greg about Rachel going away, and about taking the puppy home.

"Won't Aunt Beth find out?" said Greg.

"She hasn't yet." Ryan leaned back in the chair and yawned. It was a comfortable chair. He closed his eyes. He could have gone to sleep.

The next thing Ryan knew, Greg was shaking his arm and laughing. "What a great visitor you are!" he said. "You come to cheer up your poor, sick brother and you go straight to sleep!"

"Did I?" Ryan looked at his watch. "Help! It's six o'clock. Dad'll be waiting in the parking lot!" He grabbed his bag and stood up.

"What about this?" said Greg. He cradled the puppy in his hands.

"Give him to me." Ryan tucked the puppy into the bag and fastened the straps. "Will you be home tomorrow?"

"Hope so. In the afternoon."

"I hope so, too. I need someone to help look after this!" He patted the bag.

"Just a minute – there's something else." Greg held out a piece of wood.

"What is it? Is it Trixie's stick? The one from the beach?" He turned it over and looked at it. TRIXIE had been carved along it and colored in black.

"I brought it in with me – and my pocketknife. It's taken me most of the day. I colored it with a felt pen. Will it do for Trixie's marker – to show where...?" He couldn't say the words "buried" or "grave."

Ryan nodded. He couldn't say anything, either. The words got stuck in his throat.

Dad turned into the parking lot just as Ryan came down the steps. All the way home Ryan kept hoping they would get there before the puppy woke for its next feed. They did – just.

Dad turned on the TV to watch the news. Ryan put the bagful of puppy under his bed and hurried to the kitchen. He could see Aunt Beth through the window, carrying in some groceries from her car. He'd never have time to warm the puppy's milk before she came in. Dad might not ask any questions, but Aunt Beth would!

Ryan touched the side of the tea kettle. It was still warm. He half-filled a cup with the warm water and tiptoed away to his room. With the door shut, he pulled the bag out from under the bed and took out the can of lamb's milk. By the time he'd measured the milk powder into the water and stirred it, a few faint squeaks were coming from the bag.

It took three fills this time before the pup's appetite was satisfied. Ryan changed the paper towels and felt the hot-water bottle. It was cold again. With the pup tucked inside his shirt he sneaked into the bathroom and locked the door. He was waiting for the water to run hot when the doorknob rattled.

"Are you in there, Ryan?" It was Dad.

"Won't be long."

"Hurry. I want to wash up before dinner."

"OK."

Ryan filled the bottle and stood there. He didn't want Dad to catch him with the hot-water bottle! But, he couldn't wait in the bathroom forever. He thought of putting it inside the front of his shirt, but the pup was already there.

"Hurry up, Ryan!"

"Coming."

Ryan shoved the hot-water bottle down the back of his shorts and pulled his shirt over the top. Now he bulged at the back, as well as the front. He unlocked the door and sidled out past Dad, who watched his weird sideways walk with disbelief. A silly grin drifted across Ryan's face as he disappeared down the hall.

"That boy's behavior gets stranger every day," Ryan heard his father mutter.

When Ryan appeared in the kitchen a few minutes later, his father watched him carefully. "I'm pleased to see you walk like a human instead of a crab," he said.

Ryan's self-conscious grin came back again. He glanced at Aunt Beth. Thank goodness she was busy with her own thoughts.

After dinner Aunt Beth asked Ryan to take his bike and mail a letter for her.

"It needs to catch the eight o'clock mail," she said.

"And don't forget your helmet!"

"I never forget my helmet," Ryan said. He didn't know why she always reminded him these days. Was it because of Greg? The last time Greg hadn't worn a helmet was the time he had the accident. Ryan still couldn't understand that. Greg had never forgotten his helmet before.

He looked at his watch. He'd have to hurry to get there by eight. The puppy would sleep until he got back.

Ryan glanced at the letter as he popped it in through the slot. It was addressed to the Manager of the Riverside Retirement Home. Who did Aunt Beth know there? She wasn't thinking of retiring, was she?

Ten minutes later, as Ryan pushed his bike back up the walk, he saw Aunt Beth looking out the sunroom window – his bedroom window! Why was she in there? She *never* went in there. He'd shut the door before he left.

Ryan rushed in and stopped in the doorway. The bag was open on Ryan's bed and restless squeaks came from it. Aunt Beth had found the puppy!

Ryan pushed past her. He lifted the puppy out and cradled it against himself.

"It wants to be fed," he said. Not waiting for Aunt Beth to ask any questions, he rummaged in the bag for the eyedropper and the lamb's milk, and headed for the kitchen.

Aunt Beth followed him. She said nothing – not until the puppy was fed, its bed changed, and the hot-water bottle refilled.

"That's my hot-water bottle, I suppose," she said.

Here's where the real trouble starts, thought Ryan, and he nodded as he put the puppy into its bed.

"Does your father know about this?"

"No."

"Why didn't you tell him?"

"He would have told you, and you wouldn't have let me keep him here." Ryan stared defiantly at the floor.

"How do you know if you didn't ask?"

"Because you don't care about anything I do. I'm just a nuisance! You make a fuss over Greg, but you can't be bothered with me!" Ryan sniffed. Surely he wasn't going to cry!

"Ryan! That's not true!" Aunt Beth moved toward him, but he turned away.

"It is true. And it was your idea to make me move out of our bedroom."

"You know why we did that. There just wasn't room for all Gregory's gear," Aunt Beth objected. "He has to have his wheelchair handy, and he needs the bars so I can help him learn to walk again."

"*You* help him learn to walk?" Ryan glared at her. "He

knows you don't believe he'll ever walk again! He won't, either, while *you're* helping him."

Ryan knew immediately he'd gone too far. Aunt Beth's lips trembled and she became pale. Seconds later she was gone. Ryan heard her bedroom door slam.

Chapter 16

Ryan sat down on his bed with his back to the door. He felt cold and shaky, partly because of his words with Aunt Beth, and partly because he'd been awake half the night before. He'd never been so tired.

Dad looked into the room.

"What's going on?" he asked. "Beth's shut herself in her room and won't talk to me. You're hunched up in here. Have you been giving her a hard time again?"

"How come it is always *me* giving *her* a hard time?" Ryan muttered.

"I've told you how difficult things are for her just now..."

"Nobody cares how difficult things are for me!" Ryan stood up and swung around to face his father. "Greg's accident didn't do much for me, either!"

Dad took a step back. He'd never heard Ryan speak like that. In the silence that followed, there was a sound of rustling paper and a faint squeak. Dad pulled open the bag.

"So that's what the trouble's about!" he said. "Where did it come from?"

Ryan picked up the puppy and cradled it in one arm. He stroked it gently.

"It's Trixie's," he whispered.

"But you said she was dead."

"That's right. She is. So now there's only me to look after him. And Aunt Beth won't let me keep him. What's going to happen to him?" A tear dripped down onto the puppy's silky coat. Ryan wiped it away with his finger.

The room was silent, except for a whimper from the pup. He was sleeping, but he wriggled and whimpered again.

"He's dreaming," said Dad. "I had a dog that used to do that."

Ryan looked up suddenly. "I didn't know you had a dog. You've never talked about him."

"I didn't have him for long, and he was something I tried to forget," said Dad. Ryan could see that talking about the dog brought back unhappy memories.

"What happened?" he asked, sitting down on the bed again. Dad leaned on the windowsill.

"I was younger than you. I got him for my tenth birthday. He was a big dog, just over a year old. Part

Labrador and part German shepherd, I think. He was named Leo. I really wanted a puppy, but your grandma said she wasn't having all the problems that go along with housebreaking."

"Housebreaking isn't a problem if you go about it the right way," interrupted Ryan.

"You're probably right, but we didn't know anything about it. And that wasn't all we didn't know! We found out the rest soon enough, though."

"What do you mean?"

"We'd had him less than a week, when I heard him snarling at the mailman. He wouldn't let him near the mailbox and he wouldn't come when I called him, either. The mailman went away and we didn't get our mail. In the end I had to entice Leo into his doghouse with some meat.

"That was bad enough, but the next day when Beth came home from school, he had a cat up our plum tree. Beth called him, but he wouldn't come for her, either. She grabbed his collar to pull him away, and he sunk his teeth into her arm – up here." Dad touched his arm just below his shoulder. "It was a horrible bite. He only bit her once, but it left an ugly scar."

"I've never seen the scar," said Ryan. "Does she still have it?"

"She still has it, all right. She'll always have it. That's

why she never wears sleeveless dresses. She's never worn a swimsuit, either."

"That's horrible. What happened to Leo after that?" Ryan knew the answer to his question almost before he asked it. There is only one thing you can do with dogs that attack people. But he had to know for certain.

"My father called the dogcatcher, and he came and took Leo away. They wouldn't tell me what happened to him, but I knew they put him down." Dad was quiet for a minute.

"I suppose it's not surprising that Beth doesn't like dogs. It wasn't only the biting. Everyone felt so awful afterward. I felt guilty because it was my dog that bit Beth. My mom and dad thought it was their fault for letting me have the dog. Beth thought the dog was put down because of her, so she felt bad, too."

"But that's not all," said Aunt Beth, standing in the doorway.

Chapter 17

"I'm sorry, Aunt Beth. I'm sorry I upset you. I shouldn't have said those things." Ryan turned his head away. He thought he was going to have more trouble with tears. Now he understood why she hated dogs.

Aunt Beth shook her head.

"It's not your fault, Ryan," she said and sat on the bed beside him. She sounded quite calm and not at all upset anymore. "I've got some explaining to do – and some apologizing, too.

"I'm sorry I've neglected you this last year. I knew I was doing it, but I couldn't help myself, with Gregory's accident and all." Ryan looked surprised. "I've always loved you," she continued. "You looked so like your dad did at your age…" She was quiet for a moment. Then she went on.

"Things started to go wrong even before the accident. It was when you made plans to get a dog. Do you remember the day we went to see the puppies?"

Ryan nodded.

"Well, the mother of those puppies looked so much like Leo that the terror of that dreadful day thirty years ago came back in a great wave. As soon as my legs would work, I got out of there and locked myself in the car. I knew it was stupid, but I couldn't stop myself.

"That night I dreamed of Leo, and the cat, and the plum tree. I woke up, but the dream wouldn't go away, and I knew I couldn't live in the same house as one of those dogs."

"But Ringo wouldn't have grown up like Leo," objected Ryan.

"Maybe," said Aunt Beth. "At first I tried to persuade your father to change his mind. Forbid you to have the dog." She turned to Dad with a small, sad smile.

"You must have thought I was crazy – all the stupid reasons I had for not letting Ryan have the puppy. No wonder you didn't pay any attention.

"Then I hoped other people would buy all the pups and there wouldn't be any left. That didn't happen, either."

"You should have told me how you felt, Beth," said Dad.

Aunt Beth shrugged.

"I couldn't explain it to myself. How was I going to tell you? So, I started wishing. I wished for something to happen – I didn't care what! Anything that would stop that puppy from coming into this house." Aunt Beth hesitated. "And something did happen, didn't it?"

"What d'you mean?" Ryan looked confused.

"Gregory's accident. That's what happened. A German shepherd caused Gregory's accident." Aunt Beth twisted her hands on her lap. "That dog attacked Gregory, and gave me the excuse for not letting a dog into the house. So Gregory's accident was my fault, wasn't it? I wished for it."

"Of course it wasn't your fault!" said Dad. "The dog had nothing to do with you."

"But there's more," insisted Aunt Beth. "If Greg had worn his helmet he wouldn't have been hurt so badly."

"That was nothing to do with you, either, Aunt Beth," said Ryan. "You're always telling us to wear them."

Aunt Beth shook her head.

"Not that day," she murmured. "That was the day I told Mrs. Cooper next door about your new helmets. She wanted to show one to her husband before they bought one for Terry. I gave her Greg's. When he went to get it back, no one was home. He was only going to the corner for some milk. I told him to go without it." Her shoulders slumped.

"I didn't sleep for nights while Greg was in that coma.

When he regained consciousness and he couldn't walk, I was determined to get him walking again by myself."

She reached out and took Ryan's hand.

"I should have known you were the one who could help him most, Ryan. But because I was to blame, I had to be the one to look after him and help him walk. I couldn't think about anything else. Nothing else mattered. Not even you."

Ryan didn't know what to say. Then she let his hand go, and stood up.

"But you boys are nearly grown up now and you don't need me to look after you anymore, so I'm going at the end of the month," she said.

"Not because of what I said and not because of the puppy," said Ryan. "I promise he won't be a nuisance and," he gave a little grin, "I'll train him not to bite."

"No," said Aunt Beth, "not because of the puppy. I've been thinking about it for some time, and I made up my mind before I saw him." She leaned forward and fondled one tiny ear. Even Aunt Beth couldn't be frightened of a puppy that size.

"Gregory showed me this afternoon how you'd helped him with his walking. When I saw how quickly he was becoming independent, I decided to accept the position as Assistant Manager of the Riverside Retirement Home.

I'll take up my career where it left off six years ago."

Ryan blushed when he remembered thinking Aunt Beth might be going to retire.

"That doesn't mean you can't live here anymore," he said.

"It does mean that. It's a live-in position. An apartment comes with the job."

"You've known about this for a long time, haven't you, Dad?" Ryan turned to his father. "That's what your secret talks with Aunt Beth were about."

"Beth told me she was thinking of taking the job, and we have discussed ways of bridging the gap for awhile – until Greg's fit." He hesitated. "But the final decision was made only this afternoon."

Ryan stroked the puppy and grinned.

"Of course, Dad, you know this will mean a return to hamburgers and hot dogs!"

Chapter 18

It was three weeks before Rachel came back from her Aunt Celia's. She hurried straight around to the Lamberts, but no one answered the doorbell when she rang it.

"The van's here so someone's at home. I bet they're out on the back lawn," she muttered, as she bustled around the side of the house.

Ryan was sprawled out on the grass. Greg lazed against the trunk of the apple tree, his legs stretched out in front of him.

"Hi!" called Ryan. "Come and see this!"

The puppy wobbled around on three legs, while he hit out at Zip with his other front paw, trying to flatten her. All the time, he made little growling noises and his tail flipped from side to side, helping him keep his balance. Zip retreated just far enough to avoid the swiping paw.

"He's grown!" said Rachel. "He'll be bigger than Trixie."

"Not much bigger," grinned Ryan.

"He drinks from a bowl now," Greg boasted. "And he started on canned food yesterday."

"Come here," said Ryan. He scooped the puppy up – it took two hands now – and held him on his lap. "You're not to fight with Zip."

The puppy squirmed with delight at Ryan's attention. He wagged his tail and licked Ryan's fingers. Then, quite suddenly, he flopped down and slept. Zip crept up onto Ryan's lap, too. She curled herself around the sleeping puppy and purred.

"See," said Ryan. "We don't need a hot-water bottle anymore."

"And I don't need my wheelchair anymore – well, not *all* the time," Greg said. "I'll show you." He put his hand out to Rachel. "Help me up."

Rachel pulled him up and he steadied himself against the tree. He reached around behind it and pulled out a pair of crutches.

"Watch this," he said and, with the help of the crutches, made it to the barbecue grill and back. "And I won't need these much longer, either!"

"Great!" said Rachel. "And what's this I hear about your aunt getting a job at the retirement home?"

"That's right. She starts tomorrow."

"How will you get by without her?"

"We'll be all right," said Ryan. "Mrs. Cooper will help out with the work until Greg gets really mobile again."

"That won't be long," said Greg.

"And Aunt Beth won't be far away. She said she could be here in half an hour if we need her."

They sat quietly for a few minutes, watching Zip and the puppy sleeping on Ryan's knee.

"Are you going to get one of those German shepherds when your Aunt Beth goes?" Rachel asked.

Ryan shook his head. "No," he said.

"What about him?" Rachel pointed at the pup. "What's going to happen to him?"

"I'm going to keep him," said Ryan. "I couldn't do anything else now, could I? I wouldn't want to, anyway."

Tiny claws left pale scratches on Ryan's bare legs as the puppy grunted and wriggled to get comfortable. "And he'll be just as smart as his mother."

"What are you going to call him?" asked Rachel.

"Ringo, of course," said Ryan.

TITLES IN THE SERIES

SET 9A

Television Drama
Time for Sale
The Shady Deal
The Loch Ness Monster Mystery
Secrets of the Desert

SET 9B

To JJ From CC
Pandora's Box
The Birthday Disaster
The Song of the Mantis
Helping the Hoiho

SET 9C

Glumly
Rupert and the Griffin
The Tree, the Trunk, and the Tuba
Errol the Peril
Cassidy's Magic

SET 9D

Barney
Get a Grip, Pip!
Casey's Case
Dear Future
Strange Meetings

SET 10A

A Battle of Words
The Rainbow Solution
Fortune's Friend
Eureka
It's a Frog's Life

SET 10B

The Cat Burglar of Pethaven Drive
The Matchbox
In Search of the Great Bears
Many Happy Returns
Spider Relatives

SET 10C

Horrible Hank
Brian's Brilliant Career
Fernitickles
It's All in Your Mind,
   James Robert
Wing High, Gooftah

SET 10D

The Week of the Jellyhoppers
Timothy Whuffenpuffen-
   Whippersnapper
Timedetectors
Ryan's Dog Ringo
The Secret of Kiribu Tapu Lagoon